FOR THOSE IN PERIL

For Those in Peril

THE STORY OF
THE LIFE-BOAT SERVICE
BY MICHAEL ELDER

Eternal Father, strong to save,
Whose arm hath bound the restless wave,
Who bidd'st the mighty ocean deep
Its own appointed limits keep:
O hear us when we cry to Thee
For those in peril on the sea.
WILLIAM WHITING

John Murray
FIFTY ALBEMARLE STREET LONDON

© *Michael Elder 1963*

Printed in Great Britain by
Butler & Tanner Ltd,
Frome and London

To
SHEILA
with love

Contents

Illustrations

Illustrations

Illustrations

*Those photographs not acknowledged
in the above list belong to the Royal
National Life-boat Institution.*

FIGURES IN TEXT

Acknowledgements

A book of this kind could not be written without the help of a great number of people, and I should like to record here my gratitude to all those who have given me advice and suggestions, who have read through rough drafts of the stories and made alterations and corrections, and who have generally made the whole book possible. First and foremost I should like to thank the Royal National Lifeboat Institution for all the wonderful co-operation I have received, and in particular Mr Patrick Howarth, the Publicity Secretary, for reading the rough draft of the manuscript and for many valuable suggestions, and Miss E. M. Lloyd Jones, the Organizing Secretary for Scotland. They have answered my endless questions and requests with unbounded courtesy and patience.

I have travelled, I suppose, roughly three thousand miles with a notebook and a tape recorder to collect these stories, and I should like to thank not only those coxswains, honorary secretaries and members of life-boat crews who helped me so much and received me so cordially, who took me out on exercise in their life-boats and demonstrated their equipment, but also those who, because of time, distance and difficulties of travel, I was unable to visit, but who have been so co-operative by letter or telephone.

Among a long list of those who have helped with specific stories I should like to thank Mr Tom F. Bevan of Lynmouth; Mr E. Peter Hansell, Mr T. H. Baldwin and Coxswain Henry Davies of Cromer; Mr L. P. Stevens of St Helier, Jersey; Mr J. R. B. Harries and the members of the Selsey life-boat crew who took part in the rescue of 29 July 1956; Captain T. Stevens and Coxswain Daniel Roach of St Ives; Coxswain John Sales of Lerwick; Mr Thomas Owens, Coxswain Richard Evans and Motor Mechanic Evan Owens of Moelfre; Coxswain Sam Cunningham of Portrush; Mr W. R. Bridson of Port St Mary, Isle of Man, and Mr Robert Fraser of Aith, Shetland. To these and many others who have helped me in so many ways I am deeply grateful.

Edinburgh 1962

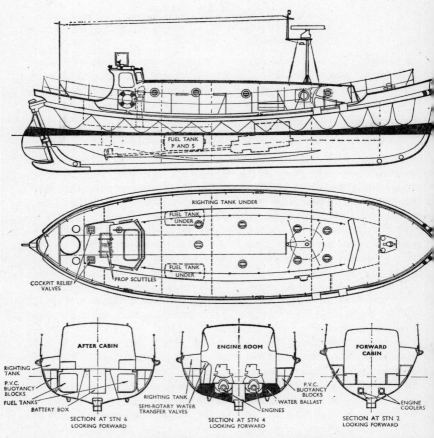

FUEL TANK
P AND S

RIGHTING TANK UNDER

FUEL TANK
UNDER

FUEL TANK
UNDER

COCKPIT RELIEF
VALVES

PROP SCUTTLES

AFTER CABIN

ENGINE ROOM

FORWARD
CABIN

RIGHTING
TANK

P.V.C.
BUOYANCY
BLOCKS

FUEL TANKS

BATTERY BOX

SECTION AT STN 6
LOOKING FORWARD

RIGHTING TANK

SEMI-ROTARY WATER
TRANSFER VALVES

ENGINES

SECTION AT STN 4
LOOKING FORWARD

WATER BALLAST

P.V.C.
BUOYANCY
BLOCKS

ENGINE
COOLERS

SECTION AT STN 2
LOOKING FORWARD

The latest addition to the life-boat fleet: the 48½ foot Oakley self-righte

CHAPTER ONE

The Story of the Life-boat

The rescue of human lives from the sea has been an exacting and heroic task ever since the first prehistoric man hollowed out a tree trunk, pushed it into the water and found that it floated. Since then there have been stories from all over the world of rescues from shipwreck which typify the courage and unselfish devotion of those who have carried out the tasks.

Perhaps nowhere in the world is the need for such rescue so acute as in the British Isles. This country is an island and our very existence depends to a large extent on our trade in shipping. To no other country, with the exception of Japan and Iceland, is the sea so important. At points all round our coast there are dangerous rocks or shifting sands, conflicting currents and treacherous tides, and although modern methods of communication, direction-finding and, more recently, echo-sounding have lessened a great many of these dangers there is not, and probably never will be, complete safety from storm and from the sea itself.

Commercial shipping has increased enormously in the past century and the need for saving lives from wrecks has not decreased. In recent years there has been a vast increase in pleasure cruising and yachting round the coast, and this has added considerably to the vital necessity of life-saving.

To combat these dangers there are several organizations whose main function it is to prevent shipwreck or to rescue those who have suffered it.

Trinity House in England, Wales and the Channel Islands, the Commissioners of Northern Lights in Scotland and the Isle of Man, and the Commissioners of Irish Lights in Northern Ireland and the Irish Republic are concerned mainly with pre-venting shipwreck. Their task is to maintain and man the hun-dreds of lighthouses and lightships round our shores, which give guidance to shipping and warning of danger.

Her Majesty's Coastguard Service keeps watch amongst other things for any ship in distress, and air-sea rescue services run by the armed forces are always ready to give assistance at sea when this is needed.

All these organizations are controlled or subsidized to some extent by the government, but the main work of rescuing lives at sea falls on an organization which receives no government support and relies entirely upon voluntary contributions to maintain its service. This is the Royal National Life-boat Institution, and it is the story of the Institution and of the men who work for it that I hope to tell something of in these pages.

It is difficult to say when a life-boat service actually came into being. The Institution itself was founded in 1824, but life-boats had been specially built and manned and had successfully carried out rescues at sea before that. In every fishing port round the coast of Britain men had always been ready to go out to the help of vessels in distress, but there was no central organization, no means of national communication, and in fact many lives were lost through this lack. Those places which had life-boat stations maintained their own boats and crews through local gifts, and were completely independent.

It is also difficult to say who built the first life-boat.

Before going any further it is important to realize exactly what a life-boat is. It is a boat designed specifically for the saving of lives, and as such rescues are usually carried out at a time when all other vessels are seeking shelter from storm and sea, it is obvious that life-boats must be of a special design. They must have great buoyancy, they must have great stability, they must have great strength and they must not lie too low in the water, for most rescues are carried out in shallow waters near the shore. Design of a life-boat differs in many respects from the design of any other type of craft.

To return to the designer of the first life-boat.

One of the candidates for this title was a London coachbuilder called Lionel Lukin who was born at Dunmow in Essex in 1742. Lukin was an inventor, besides carrying out his ordinary trade, and one of his experiments was converting a Norway yawl to make it—as he himself put it—'unimmergible'. He was not concerned at that time with making a life-boat as such, but merely a boat which would not sink. His design had several unusual features. One of them was a projecting cork gunwale, nine inches thick amidships, tapering towards the stem and stern. Another was a watertight compartment for extra buoyancy built into the boat, and two further watertight compartments at the stem and stern. He also incorporated a false iron keel under the boat which added weight below water and helped to keep the boat upright. He converted two boats in this way, but although both appear to have fulfilled their purpose in bad weather sailing, neither of them was ever used for life-saving. However, news of his experiments reached the ears of a certain Dr John Sharp, Archdeacon of Northumberland.

Dr Sharp was the chief administrator of a Trust known as the Crewe Trust which had been established at Bamburgh in Northumberland after the death of the third Baron Crewe, Bishop of Durham, in 1721. This Trust carried out many charitable works, one of which was to assist in life-saving from shipwrecks. Through the years an extremely efficient organization for sea rescue was built up, and when in 1786 Dr Sharp heard of Lukin's experiments he asked Lukin to convert a small coble according to his new designs, and this Lukin did. The converted coble was returned to Bamburgh and served there for many years. So Bamburgh can claim to be the first life-boat station in Britain, possibly in the world.

After this Lukin spent a lot of time developing life-boats. He died at the age of ninety-one and on his tombstone were engraved the words he himself asked for:

'This Lionel Lukin was the first to build a life-boat.'

This claim is all very well, but it is somewhat sweeping. There is another candidate who did as much as Lukin did, and it is through this man we can see that the problems of saving life from the sea were being studied not only in Britain but in other parts of the world. A Frenchman named Bernières designed a boat which would not sink when swamped or overloaded. Bernières was Director of the Bridges and Causeways of France and his first experiments, begun as early as 1765, culminated in a trial on 1 August 1777 on the Seine at Paris. His design, however, was for a boat mainly using inland waterways, and there is no evidence that his boat was actually used for saving life.

Besides Lukin and Bernières there are other candidates for the honour of inventing the first life-boat.

In 1789 the *Adventurer*, a Newcastle ship, went aground on the Herd Sands at the entrance to the river Tyne in a gale. The crew retreated before the lashing seas into the rigging, and one by one, as exhaustion and exposure overcame them, they dropped off, in full view of a crowd of people watching helplessly from the shore only a few hundred yards away. All the crew were drowned. It is obvious that even at this time some serious thought was being given in certain quarters to the problem of rescuing sailors from shipwreck, because the members of a private club in South Shields who called themselves the Gentlemen of the Lawe House, offered a prize of two guineas for the best design for a life-boat, and there were a number of entries.

The winner was William Wouldhave, a parish clerk in South Shields, who claimed that he had got the idea for his design during a country stroll when he had stopped to watch a woman drawing water in a dipper from a well. This dipper was a curved vessel, remarkable because however it was put into the water it always came up upright. Wouldhave designed a life-boat on the same principle and won the award. This was in many ways the forerunner of the self-righting life-boat. We shall find out more about self-righters later.

When Wouldhave died in 1820 his tombstone was inscribed:

'Inventor of that invaluable blessing to man, the Life-boat.'

These men, then, claim to have invented the life-boat, but there is another candidate.

Although Wouldhave won the award offered for a life-boat design by the Gentlemen of the Lawe House, his design cannot altogether have satisfied them, because they cut the prize by a half and only gave Wouldhave a guinea. There is a story that Wouldhave flung the guinea down in disgust when the announcement was made, but this has never been verified. Certainly it was not Wouldhave's design which was finally built.

Two members of the Gentlemen of the Lawe House named

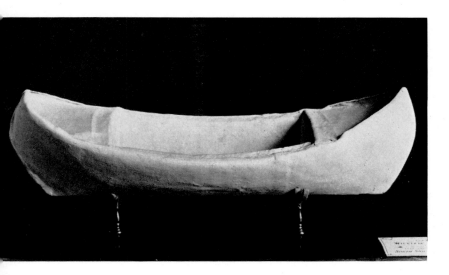

The model of a life-saving boat submitted for the Gentlemen of the Lawe House's competition by William Wouldhave in 1789. See page 4

Henry Greathead's *Original*, the first life-boat specially built for the purpose, launched in January 1790. See page 5

Horses were used to launch life-boats as late as 1934. This is the
Brooke, Isle of Wight, life-boat with her launching team

The fore part of the s.s. *Rohilla*, aground on Saltwick Nab, Whitby,
in 1914. Altogether six life-boats took part in the rescue of the
survivors. See Chapter III

Fairles and Rockwood took it upon themselves to study all the designs submitted for the contest, and from these designs they modified Wouldhave's original plan. They built another model and ordered a boat to be built from it.

The man who built this boat was Henry Greathead, a South Shields shipbuilder who was born in Richmond in Yorkshire.

The boat was launched on 30 January 1790, and was called, appropriately and prophetically, the *Original*. It was the first life-boat designed and built specifically for the purpose, 30 feet long with six pairs of oars for pulling, cork-lined for buoyancy, with a cork fender outside. She was in service for forty years and saved hundreds of lives.

The launching of the first life-boat attracted considerable attention, and Greathead became famous. He was given £1,200 by Parliament, a hundred guineas by Trinity House, and other awards, some of them from abroad. And he received an award of a hundred guineas from Lloyd's, the shipping insurers, who were not unnaturally extremely interested in life-boat construction. Furthermore, Lloyd's paid Greathead to build a number of other similar boats, and by 1803 he had built thirty-one of them.

These are the men who can lay claim to designing and building the first life-boat. Perhaps it is fairest to say that the credit should go to all three.

So by the start of the nineteenth century life-boats were beginning to appear, but for some years yet they were only maintained by local contributions at different places round the shores of Britain. Isolated and unconnected, they worked independently of each other, and although these local stations did some magnificent work, the overall effect was not satisfactory. For the beginning of a national organization to control these different efforts we have to go to the Isle of Man.

In 1802 one of Henry Greathead's life-boats was ordered by the Duke of Atholl and sent to Douglas on the Isle of Man. Douglas, situated on the island in the middle of the Irish Sea, had witnessed a large number of shipwrecks and much loss of life, and a life-boat was clearly a necessity. One of the members of the new life-boat's crew was Sir William Hillary.

Hillary had had an active life. Born in 1771 he had travelled extensively, and had a fortune from sugar plantations in the West Indies which he lost when the plantations failed. He raised a legion of some 1,400 men during the Napoleonic Wars for home defence. He financed this venture and commanded the legion himself, and for his services to his country he was made a baronet in 1805. He wrote a number of pamphlets advocating many different things. All his writings were fired with common sense and a great deal of imagination, and it was one of these pamphlets which gave rise to the founding of the Royal National Life-boat Institution. It was called *An Appeal to the British Nation on the Humanity and Policy of forming a National Institution for the Preservation of Lives and Property from Shipwreck.* A second edition of this pamphlet appeared in London in 1824.

It aroused such interest and enthusiasm that within a year the National Institution for the Preservation of Life from Shipwreck had been formed under the patronage of King George IV and the presidency of the Prime Minister, the Earl of Liverpool, with the support of the Dukes of York, Sussex, Clarence and Cambridge, the Archbishops of Canterbury and York, and many other distinguished churchmen, naval officers and Members of Parliament. This in itself shows the strength of Hillary's writings and the national need for such an institution. At a meeting held in the London Tavern on 12 February 1824 his recommendations were unanimously approved, and at a further meeting on 4 March the Institution was born.

The suggestions put forward by Hillary in his pamphlet have almost all been incorporated in the organization of the Institution as it is today, and this is another proof of his far-sightedness. Among the things which he advocated and which are still in force are the following: that the Institution should be supported by voluntary contributions; suitable rewards should be paid to those who carried out rescues; provision should be made for widows and dependants of those who lost their lives in the service; the conferring of awards for gallantry; and finally 'The people and vessels of every nation, whether in peace or war, shall be equal objects of this Institution.'

Hillary himself served for many years with the Douglas life-boat, saving 300 lives and winning the Institution's gold medal three times, a feat which has since been equalled but not exceeded. The gold medal, awarded for 'great gallantry', is the Institution's equivalent of the Victoria Cross. It also awards silver and bronze medals for outstanding services.

In 1847 Hillary died in poverty at Douglas, but the Institution which he started lives after him.

But although great interest was shown at the founding of the Institution in 1824 it did not last very long. The problem of

... affected many people
... their living in ships of all
... the coast where wrecks
... ast majority of the popu-
... Shipwreck Institution.
... o radio, and newspapers
... which they have today.
... g out how other people
... Institution, which had
... on found it difficult to
... ich it was formed.
... lation of the Institution
... change this.

... rescue from the *Forfar-*
... s effects on the attitude
... story briefly once again.
... r of Waterloo, 1815, at
... Darling who became
... 1826 on Longstone, one

... Darling was twenty-two
... om the south-south-east.
... e Longstone lighthouse,
... had gone ashore on a
... clear he would not be
... so Grace and her father
... nall, open boat usually
... me had been exception-

The *Forfarshire* was a paddle steamer, the pride of her owners. She was on her regular passage from Hull to Dundee on this night with sixty-three people on board.

7

During the night the gale backed to the north and strengthened considerably, and the *Forfarshire* sprang a leak in her boiler which could not be controlled and rendered her engine useless. The captain decided to shelter among the Farne Islands until the gale moderated, but somehow he mistook his course and the steamer struck a rock near the Longstone lighthouse and immediately broke in two.

Almost all the passengers on this luxury steamer were swept out to sea and drowned, but thirteen of them reached the rock, some of them very badly injured. Amongst these thirteen was a mother with her two children.

Grace Darling, looking out of her bedroom window in the early hours of the morning, saw the tangled wreck of the *Forfarshire* being pounded on the rocks. She called her father, and immediately the two Darlings set out to the rescue. This was a normal part of a lightkeeper's duties in those days, and had Grace's brother been present he would undoubtedly have gone instead. As it was, Grace went with her father. The gale was such that they were sure no boat could reach the wreck from the shore. The only hope for any survivors there might be was for Grace and her father to make for the scene of the wreck in their coble.

Although the wreck was only three hundred yards away they had to row for nearly a mile to reach it, and when they drew near they saw that there were more survivors than their coble could safely hold. Nine people were now left on the rock. The two children and two of the adults had died before the Darlings could reach them. Grace and her father took off five of the survivors including the mother of the children. This was all their coble could hold, and they returned to the lighthouse with them. There Grace looked after them while her father, with two of the men they had brought off, who were members of the *Forfarshire*'s crew, returned for the remainder.

Half an hour after the last survivors were taken off the rock the North Sunderland life-boat reached the scene, having managed to launch against all the odds. One of the members of the crew was Grace's brother William.

This was a major disaster which punctured the assured life of the British public of the time, and it was not until some days later that Grace Darling's part in the rescue became known. Then the publicity broke, and overnight Grace Darling, much against her will, found herself famous. The story of the twenty-two-year-old girl who had set out on such a night to rescue survivors from shipwreck stirred the imagination of the country, and Grace Darling became a national heroine.

But she did not enjoy this doubtful pleasure for long. Four years later she contracted tuberculosis and she died on 24 October 1842 at the age of twenty-six. At Bamburgh, the first life-boat station in the world, there is a plaque on the Post Office wall which says that Grace Darling died in that house.

Her action was certainly a brave one, but she herself could never really understand the fuss that was made about it. It seemed to her to be out of all proportion to the act itself. She did not relish publicity, and as the daughter of a lighthouse-keeper she had merely helped her father to perform a duty which he undertook in the normal course of his working life, but the effect of her action was to create a greater interest in the problem of saving life at sea, and this was of benefit to the Shipwreck Institution.

The organization changed its name to the Royal National Life-boat Institution in 1854, and some measure of the work it has done can be gained from the fact that from the time of its formation to the present day it has saved nearly 85,000 lives.

The first life-boats, as we have seen, were manned by crews pulling oars. Then masts were added and sails could be used when the weather allowed, so the life-boat had two sources of power—oars and sail. These were the pulling and sailing life-boats. Steam life-boats were used for a time, but these were generally found to be unsatisfactory for several different reasons which we shall see later. Motor life-boats are now in use at all life-boat stations, and these are of several different types.

The physical layout of different life-boat stations makes it impossible to stick to any one particular design. Some stations are in remote areas where a big life-boat has to be used because of the great distances she may have to cover. Others are launched into shallow water where the draft and weight of the bigger boats would render it impossible to launch except at certain stages of the tide. Some boats lie afloat in harbours, some are pulled over beaches into the water by tractors, others are launched down slipways from boathouses.

Modern life-boats range in size from the Barnett, which is 52 feet long, has a crew of eight and a radius of action at full speed without refuelling of 180 miles, to the Oakley which is 48½ feet long, has a crew of seven and a radius of action of 72 miles. The Barnett can carry 100 people in rough weather, the Oakley 35. The R.N.L.I. at present builds six different types of life-boat. Apart from the Barnett and the Oakley these are the 47-foot Watson, the 42-foot Watson, and the 42-foot Beach life-boat and the newly introduced 48½-foot Oakley. Life-boats themselves are usually named after the people or organizations which provide the money for them.

If a life-boatman of the last century could see a modern life-boat he would be amazed at the number of aids carried which were unknown in his day. His work was the back-breaking task of rowing a heavy life-boat through wind and sea, guided only by flares sent up by the vessel he was making for if it was dark, otherwise mainly by guesswork.

And yet the life-boatman of the last century would be the first to realize that although all these modern aids have improved the life-boat's chances of success in a rescue, the dangers which have always been present are as great as they have ever been. The life-boat service today is working harder than ever before, and because of these new aids, saving more lives than ever before. But that does not mean that the work is any less arduous or any safer. Life-boatmen still risk their lives every time they go out on service, and sometimes lives are lost. On 9 February 1953 the Fraserburgh life-boat, escorting fishing vessels into Fraserburgh harbour in a storm, capsized. Only one man of her crew of seven was saved. That man was the second coxswain. He became second coxswain on the new life-boat, while the new coxswain is the brother of the coxswain who lost his life. On 8 December 1959 the Broughty Ferry life-boat answered a call by the Carr Rocks lightship off Fife Ness. The lightship was reported to be dragging her cable and drifting in a gale. Somewhere on the way the life-boat capsized with the loss of her entire crew. Yet a fortnight later when a reserve life-boat arrived at Broughty Ferry, forty applications were received by the honorary secretary from men who wished to serve with the new crew.[1]

What is it that makes a man volunteer for this arduous and dangerous task? It is difficult to say. In some cases it is a family tradition. In others it is perhaps simply the seafaring spirit of a nation which recognizes the constant danger of the sea and the deep-felt human desire to help others in distress. Whatever it is no one can doubt that it is a quality which has been in the British race for many centuries, and which is as strong today as it has ever been.

And who are these men who go out on service in the life-boats? The answer is, almost anybody. True, most crews are made up of inshore fishermen and others who earn their living from the sea, because they must have an expert and complete knowledge of the waters they are sailing in. But there are life-boat stations which have coal-miners and doctors and many other trades and professions amongst their crews.

These men are unpaid. Their work is voluntary. The Royal National Life-boat Institution makes money awards to life-boat crews when they go out on exercise or are called out on service and they receive retaining fees, but there is no regular wage for the work they do. Only the motor mechanic, whose duty it is to see that the life-boat is ready at all times to go to sea, has a full-time job and receives a wage. The rest of the crew, the honorary secretary of each life-boat station and the many helpers who are needed ashore to launch the life-boat, give their services willingly and freely.

This is perhaps the most remarkable thing about the Royal National Life-boat Institution. About 150 life-boats are kept constantly ready all round the coast of Great Britain and Ireland, besides a reserve fleet of boats ready to replace a boat which may suffer damage on service, which happens frequently, or require an overhaul. The cost of running the Institution is

---

[1] A week after the manuscript for this book was finished the Seaham, County Durham, life-boat, with only five of her normal crew of eight, went to the assistance of a fishing coble, *Economy*. She took four men and a nine-year-old boy off the coble, but returning to Seaham Harbour the life-boat *George Elmy* capsized. Only one of *Economy*'s crew, the boy's father, survived. Everyone else was drowned.

over a million pounds a year, yet all this money is raised voluntarily. Not a single penny comes from the government. This is with the full approval of all political parties and the Institution itself. For a time, from 1854 when the Institution was in serious financial difficulties, the government did make a grant, but this meant a measure of control over the running of the Institution which seriously hampered its work, and in 1869 the grant was withdrawn. Since then the Institution has been dependent on voluntary subscriptions, bequests and legacies, and the proceeds of the Flag Days which are held all over the country. It seems unbelievable that some local councils still refuse to allow the R.N.L.I. to hold a Flag Day.

The R.N.L.I. today is a highly organized, well-run concern. Each life-boat station has its honorary secretary who is responsible for the general administration of the station and who is also responsible for deciding when the life-boat should be launched on service. He works in close contact with the coxswain who is in charge of the life-boat itself. Besides the coxswain, the crew consists of the second coxswain, motor mechanic, assistant motor mechanic, bowman, signalman and two or three crewmen, depending on the size of life-boat. Most calls for the life-boat come from the coastguard stations round Britain and these messages are sent straight to the honorary secretary. The crew is summoned as soon as the honorary secretary, in consultation with the coxswain, has decided that the life-boat may have to be launched. This is usually done by firing the maroons, and when the members of the crew hear it they immediately leave whatever task they are engaged on and make for the life-boat station on foot, on bicycle or by car. The shore helpers gather, too. The life-boat is launched from the boathouse at some stations, down a slipway straight into the water. At others, a heavy, watertight tractor tows it across the beach and pushes it into the sea on a carriage. Some are moored in harbours and the crews reach them in special boarding boats. Others lie at quaysides and all the crew have to do is to slip their cables and they are ready to go. At two stations in Britain the life-boat is kept on the beach and is pushed into the water on skids. From the time the message is received to the time of launch is usually a matter of minutes.

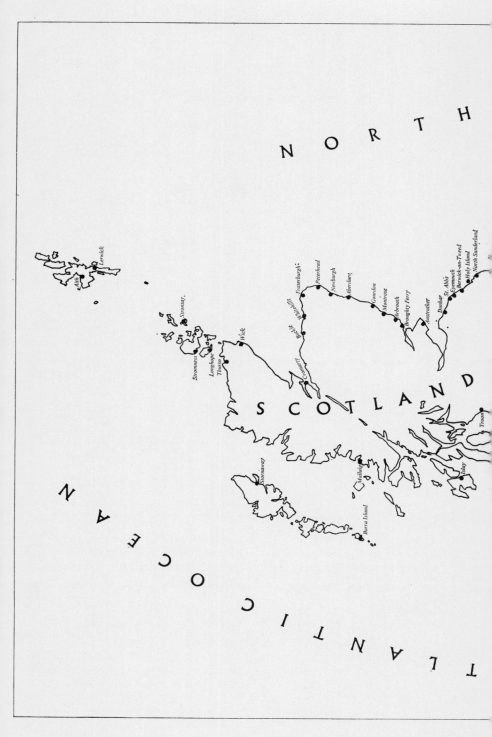

NORTH

ATLANTIC OCEAN

SCOTLAND

Lerwick

Fitlar

Stronsay

Stromness
Longhope
Thurso

Wick

Cromarty

Balintore
Whitehills

Fraserburgh
Peterhead

Newburgh

Aberdeen

Gourdon
Montrose
Arbroath
Broughty Ferry

Anstruther

Dunbar
St. Abbs
Eyemouth
Berwick-on-Tweed
Holy Island
North Sunderland

Stornaway

Mallaig

Barra Island

Islay

Troon

Not all calls come from vessels in distress. The life-boat service has many other calls made on it, and in the stories which follow I have tried to give as varied a picture of the Institution's work as I can.

When I first began research for this book the biggest difficulty was the selection of material for the stories. Not because there was not enough. There was far too much. The daily stories of gallantry and heroism become almost commonplace as you read through report after report. I decided to observe two principles. One was that the stories I selected should give as widely differing a picture of the work of the Institution as possible, not only at the present time, but in the past as well. The other was to cover life-boat stations all over the British Isles. Therefore there are stories from Lerwick in Shetland to St Ives in Cornwall; from Arranmore on the west coast of Eire to Cromer in Norfolk. There are stories of courage and endurance which I have had to miss out simply because there was not space, but I should like to make it clear that the stories in this book have not been selected because they show more heroism or endurance than any others. It is simply that each story helps to show a different aspect of the Institution's work. Most of them take place in different parts of the country, and if they serve to give a general picture of the work which the life-boat service as a whole is carrying out twenty-four hours a day, 365 days a year, then my main purpose has been achieved.

It seems appropriate to end this chapter by quoting the words used about the life-boat by one of the greatest Englishmen of all time, Sir Winston Churchill.

' . . . it drives on with a mercy which does not quail in the presence of death, it drives on as a proof, a symbol, a testimony, that man is created in the image of God, and that virtue and valour have not perished from the British race.'

CHAPTER TWO

Lynmouth—1899

The modern diesel-driven, twin-engined life-boat is the natural development of the first life-boats, but throughout the history of that development a vast amount of change and experiment has taken place. A life-boat is not something which can be put together lightly, nor can its design be left in any way to chance or to luck. On the seaworthiness and handling capacity of the boat depend not only the lives of the crew but also the lives of those whom the crew set out to rescue.

Perhaps the most important single necessity in a life-boat is stability. The crew must have the utmost confidence in the ability of their boat to stay afloat in the worst imaginable conditions.

Now the finest examples of stability in shipping go back over a thousand years. The old Viking longboats which ravaged the shores of Britain long before the Norman Conquest were perhaps the most seaworthy vessels ever designed. In these longboats the old Norseman had sailed the stormy northern seas and reached out as far as America, and through the following centuries the general plan of the Viking ships has been followed by many people. These longboats had flat bottoms, were high and rounded at stem and stern, and the midships section was very similar to the early life-boats. They had banks of oars for rowing and a huge oar astern for steering. They carried an enormous sail. In Scandinavia the direct descendant of the longboat was the Norway yawl, and it was a Norway yawl that Lukin used to convert into the first 'unimmergible' boat.

Of course, in the days before the Royal National Life-boat Institution took over the running of a national life-boat service, boats used for life-saving stationed at different places round the coast varied according to the type of boat in general use at these stations. Therefore the types of boats used for life-saving in

Norfolk and Suffolk differed greatly from those used in Cornwall or Devon, and the boats used in Orkney and Shetland bore a closer resemblance to the Scandinavian boats than those of Wales or Sussex, because the connexion between Norway and those northern islands has always been very strong.

But these early boats were usually used for other purposes besides saving life at sea, and it was only slowly that a boat designed specifically for that purpose emerged. Even then the design varied according to where the boat was stationed—whether it would have to contend with wrecks stranded on sandbanks or driven ashore amongst rocks, whether the station stood on a shelving beach or at the foot of towering cliffs.

Lukin's 'unimmergible' boat and Greathead's *Original* had many similar features, although both boats were designed independently. The *Original* had six thwarts and, being very broad, these seated two men each, so that she was propelled by twelve oarsmen. She was clearly a satisfactory design, for she remained in service for forty years before she was lost at the mouth of the Tyne where she had worked for so long.

Greathead, as we have seen, built over thirty similar lifeboats which found their way to various places round the coast of Britain. Some were sent abroad, so the conception of lifesaving services in other countries was growing at the same time, and it was from these boats that many of the features of the later life-boats were taken.

Sails were introduced, and the later life-boats carried two short masts, which could be raised and lowered when necessary, and the rig was lugsails and a small jib. The number of men used to row the boat depended on the size and weight of the boat itself, but was usually either ten or twelve.

Life-boat work in those early days must indeed have been a backbreaking job, for propelling a heavy boat through mountainous seas for hours at a time was no job for weaklings. Furthermore there was no shelter of any kind in these early lifeboats, and the crew were at all times exposed to the weather. This meant that frequently the crew would arrive at the wreck they were trying to reach in an exhausted state—the very time when they should have been alert and fresh for the most difficult part of their work.

There were two big problems in life-boat work in those early days. The first was the problem of communication. Nowadays a vessel in trouble can radio for help. The call is picked up by the coastguard or by G.P.O. radio stations and relayed to the honorary secretary by telephone. The life-boat can be launched within minutes of the call. In the early days much depended on the vigilance and good eyesight of the coastguard. If the weather was clear he might see a ship in distress, but most wrecks occur either in bad visibility or in darkness, and in these cases the coastguard of the last century could only pick up distress flares to show him that something was wrong. Even then he might not know exactly what was the matter or where the casualty might be lying. Once he became aware of a ship in trouble he still had to communicate with the honorary secretary of the life-boat station and someone had to carry the message.

Once the message was received at the life-boat station the second problem arose. This was launching the life-boat. In those days most boathouses stood on beaches and the life-boat stood on a carriage inside. When the call came a team of horses was harnessed to the carriage and the life-boat was dragged down the beach to the sea. Then the carriage was turned and hundreds of shore helpers assisted in pushing it into the sea. In bad conditions the shore helpers were frequently submerged up to their necks before the life-boat was safely on its way, and there are cases on record of shore helpers, and horses too, being swept out to sea and drowned. The crew were already in their places, their oars held upright waiting to set off the moment the word came. The life-boat slipped off the carriage into the surf, and when the coxswain gave the order the crew dipped their oars as one man and began to pull like maniacs to drive through the surf into the deeper water beyond. Once clear of the surf, if the weather permitted the sail could be hoisted, but it was in the surf that many life-boat launches failed. Often the strength of the sea was such that no human power could propel the life-boat away from the shore, and there are cases where the crew had to be brought ashore themselves, almost unable to walk from their efforts, and the life-boat had never even reached deep water. Very often a launch near the boathouse was impossible because of the state of the tide or the wind blowing directly on to the shore from the sea.

On these occasions it was necessary to take the life-boat to a place where there might be enough shelter to enable the boat to get away. Sometimes this was in a sheltered cove at the foot of a cliff where a path down to the shore could not be tackled by horses, and the life-boat would be dragged on these occasions, a ponderous, sluggish, obstinate brute of a thing on land, by hundreds of men, and often by women and children as well.

Perhaps one of the most remarkable examples of this type of launch happened at Lynmouth.

Lynmouth is a seaside resort well known to holidaymakers. Overlooking the Bristol Channel, crouched at the foot of the high hills of Exmoor, it is a place full of visitors in the summer, the little harbour is packed with pleasure craft, and the shops are gay with colourful picture postcards and souvenirs.

It used to be an important harbour for trading vessels, but these days are gone now. A life-boat station was established at Lynmouth in 1869, but there is no station there today. It was closed shortly after the last war when bigger life-boats with a wider operational range were stationed at Ilfracombe to the west and Minehead to the east. The old life-boat-house stood just to the west of the harbour, and you can still see the gateway in the wall bordering the road by the sea through which the life-boat was dragged on to the shore for launching.

It was here in 1899 that one of the most extraordinary life-boat launches took place, an epic story which is without parallel in life-boat history and a tribute to the courage and endurance of the life-boatmen of the time.

On the night of 12 January 1899 a ferocious gale was blowing from the west, a gale which swept the sea over the harbour and the sea front in a mass of tortured spray. At seven o'clock that evening the honorary secretary of the Lynmouth Life-boat Station, the Rev. A. R. Hockley, received a telegram from Porlock Weir to say that a large vessel was drifting ashore and sending up distress signals. Porlock Weir is some ten miles to the east of Lynmouth, and from the telegram the honorary secretary realized that the vessel, whatever it was, was in great danger of running ashore.

He consulted Coxswain John Crocombe. The conditions were such that the life-boat could never be launched from Lynmouth. No crew could ever pull the boat through the seas breaking on the shore.

It was learnt afterwards that the life-boat station at Ilfracombe had also seen this same vessel some time earlier and had been unable to launch to help it.

However, it took more than these circumstances to make the life-boatmen admit defeat, and in this case defeat was never contemplated. The vessel in distress was at Porlock Bay. There might be sufficient shelter in Porlock Bay to launch the life-boat. Porlock Bay was ten miles away, the gale was still blowing, even stronger than before, the route by land was perhaps one of the most difficult in the whole country, but without hesitation the coxswain suggested that the life-boat should be taken overland to Porlock Bay in the hope of launching there. With this suggestion the honorary secretary immediately agreed.

They tried to contact Porlock by telegraph to learn some more details, but by now the gale had blown the wires down somewhere between Porlock and Lynmouth and further communication was impossible. They did not know the exact position of the vessel in distress, they did not even know whether it would be possible to launch the life-boat into Porlock Bay. They had received the one brief message and then there was silence.

On the face of it, it was an impossible task from the very beginning. To start with, the road to Porlock was too narrow in parts for the life-boat carriage to get through, and furthermore the journey would mean pulling the life-boat on its carriage up a hill rising one foot in every four—one of the steepest roads in the country—crossing ten miles of wind-swept moorland, and then descending another hill of one in four into Porlock at the other end. It was a task which Hercules would have thought about twice before attempting it.

The coxswain explained his idea to the second coxswain, G. S. Richards. The second coxswain agreed.

The crowds had assembled at the life-boathouse as they

always did when news came of a vessel in distress and help was needed. These people lent their help willingly and eagerly to launch the life-boat whenever it was necessary; their one thought at such times was to do all in their power to save lives in danger from the sea, but when the idea was put to them many people there were aghast. They knew what a journey to Porlock with the life-boat would mean. It was a journey to tax the strongest heart and the stoutest body in good weather. To drag the life-boat there in the gale which was then blowing was impossible. It was not that they were unwilling to make the attempt. It was simply that they were convinced that such an attempt was bound to fail.

However, the coxswain had suggested the idea, the second coxswain had agreed with it, and the honorary secretary had given his approval. These were the men who made the decisions and whose orders were to be obeyed.

Preparations were made to go to the help of a vessel about which they knew next to nothing, which might already be a total wreck by the time they arrived, which might have drifted for miles before they could launch, and about which they were unable to get any further information. Yet they went.

A horse and cart were obtained, and seven men went ahead with it, taking with them pick-axes and shovels and wooden skids. With the picks and shovels they were to dig in the ditches at the sides of the road and widen the banks where they were too narrow for the life-boat carriage to pass. They took the skids because there were places where the carriage could not get through and the life-boat would have to be slid along on its own. This cart went on ahead.

Twenty horses were borrowed. They were harnessed to the huge, unwieldy looking life-boat carriage on which the life-boat *Louisa* was set. She had a crew of thirteen, ten of them oarsmen. At eight o'clock the impossible journey began.

The horses were unused to pulling together in such a large team, but with the aid of the men and women helpers who had assembled, the procession moved slowly out of Lynmouth and faced the first enormous obstacle: Countisbury Hill, rising one thousand feet in about a mile to the Exmoor heights. The road was narrow. The carriage only just fitted in between the banks.

For Those in Peril

The horses sweated and strained in their harness, the helpers hauled on the drag ropes, and slowly the carriage with the life-boat on it creaked and groaned its way up that terrible slope and reached the top. And then one of the wheels of the carriage came off. It had been bumped and scraped against the bank so much on the way up that it had become loose.

The helpers gathered round and raised the life-boat carriage sufficiently to allow the wheel to be replaced. A new pin to hold it in position was produced and the procession moved on once more.

Now they were on the top of the hill, exposed to the full fury of the wind and the rain. The gale which had been fierce enough in Lynmouth was ten times worse up here on the open moor. They had oil lanterns and flares for lights, but most of them were soon blown out and could not be relit in the gale.

Here many of the helpers refused to go on. The journey had been impossible from the start, they said, and now they could go no further. Some of them turned back, but the coxswain urged the others to carry on, and many of them did.

Soon after this they caught up with the horse and cart which had gone ahead. They had been digging in the ditches and widening the banks as they went to give the carriage room to get through. Now there was little more they could do. They had reached Ashton Lane, and here the road was only seven feet wide in places and the carriage could not possibly get through.

Again it looked as if the attempt must fail, but Jack Crocombe, the coxswain, said they had come so far and they were not going to be defeated now.

There were narrow gate posts at the entrance to the lane, and these were dug out. The life-boat was manhandled off its carriage and the quieter horses were selected to pull it through the lane, because without its carriage the life-boat would be as unwieldy as a whale on dry land. The carriage itself was sent round with the other horses to meet up with the life-boat half a mile further on. This route, although longer, was easier without the weight of the life-boat.

This was where the skids played their part. These were long thin wooden strips which were placed on the ground for the keel of the life-boat to be dragged over, but progress was pain-

The Always Ready, the Runswick life-boat in which Coxswain
Robert Patton lost his life. See chapter IV

A later life-boat entirely power-driven. The Arranmore, County
Donegal, life-boat puts to sea

After three days at sea the Ballycotton life-boat takes the crew off the drifting Daunt Rock lightship. See chapter v

fully slow because the life-boat could only go a certain distance before it had to be stopped to allow the men to gather the skids which the life-boat had passed over and carry them ahead of the life-boat to put down again. The road was so narrow that the men engaged on this work had great difficulty in passing between the boat and the bank.

And still the gale was howling round them and the rain stung their faces as though nature itself was determined that this attempt should fail.

At last they were through the lane and met with the carriage again. The life-boat was lifted on to the carriage and they staggered on through that night of torment.

And now came another dreadful difficulty. They had climbed the steep slope of Countisbury Hill. Now they had to go down Porlock Hill which was just as steep, and they had a load which was heavier than anything which had ever been known to go down the hill before. Drag ropes were hitched to hold the carriage back and all the men took the strain on them. Safety chains were put on the wheels and the life-boat was lashed to her carriage. But if the ropes holding her broke, or the life-boat worked loose with the bumping and swaying she was receiving, the whole contraption would career down the hill and smash to pieces at the foot. . . .

However, they reached the bottom without mishap. At the foot of the hill were some old cottages and the road turned sharply. The turn was too sharp for the life-boat to go round, so the men began to knock down the garden wall to make room for it.

The old lady who owned the cottage heard the noise and came out to ask indignantly what they thought they were doing, knocking down her wall at that time of night. The men shouted an explanation to her above the howling of the wind: there was a ship in distress in Porlock Bay and they had brought the life-boat to Porlock from Lynmouth to launch it and go to her aid.

Although she lived so near the sea the old lady had never seen a life-boat before, and when she heard their story she helped the men to knock down her own wall, and she went along with them to help them on their journey.

The life-boat was eased round the bend and continued on her way. A little later lights loomed up through the squalls of rain ahead of them and they met some men who had come to meet them from Porlock Weir.

The news they brought seemed to be the last straw.

The sea had washed away the wall and parts of the main road, and this was now impassable. There only remained a small higher road.

There was no point in turning back now that they had come so far, so the tired men and exhausted horses dragged the carriage along this smaller road.

Their troubles were not yet over. At one point a laburnum tree grew at the side of the road, and its branches hung so low that the life-boat could not pass underneath. The men sawed the tree down.

Some time later they reached Porlock. The journey of one and a half miles up Countisbury hill, ten miles across the moor and one and a half miles down Porlock Hill had taken them ten and a half hours, and at six in the morning, without even waiting for food, the life-boat crew took their places in the life-boat. Soaked, hungry and desperately tired after their nightmare journey they seized their oars, the life-boat was safely launched, and they began to pull her through the mountainous seas.

They found the ship in distress. She was the *Forest Hall*, a full-rigged ship of 1,900 tons. She had been in the tow of a tug from Bristol bound for Liverpool when the gale had sprung up the previous day and her tow rope had parted. She had drifted all night before the wind with her anchors both down and her rudder damaged, and when the life-boat found her she was perilously close to the shore. The life-boat stood by her in case the situation became so desperate that the captain decided to abandon ship, but just as dawn was breaking a tug was seen approaching and the life-boat passed a line from the tug to the *Forest Hall*. Some of the life-boat crew went aboard the vessel to help raise the anchors, and the life-boat stayed with her while she was towed to Barry on the Welsh coast.

At Barry Docks the crew were given dry clothes and food by the Shipwrecked Mariners' Society. They reached Barry at six o'clock in the evening, and the food was the first they had had for over twenty-four hours. The following day a steamer gave them a tow back to Lynmouth.

That is the story of one of the most fantastic launches in the history of the life-boat service. The youngest member of the crew that day was Mr W. H. Richards, brother of the second coxswain and later to become second coxswain himself. He was sixteen.

Mr Tom F. Bevan, the ex-honorary secretary of the Lynmouth life-boat station, introduced me to ex-Second Coxswain Richards at the end of the new car park in Lynmouth on the bank of the river which a few years ago overflowed and flooded a large part of the town. Mr Richards was engaged with brush and paint pot, touching up the woodwork of a small rowing boat. I asked him about this epic launch and he treated my enquiries with a kind of amused and half-impatient tolerance.

'Why does everyone want to make a story of that?' he asked. 'It was all just part of the job in those days.'

Mr Richards is now over eighty years old, but he still has that indefinable air of youth which seems miraculously to cling to life-boatmen. He is not so concerned with that service as he is with the fact that the Lynmouth station is now closed. This, he feels, was a mistake on the part of the Institution, and that some day they will regret it. He explained his reasons for thinking so with a wealth of precise information about currents, tides and wind directions and velocities in the Lynmouth area which I found fascinating.

Whether the Institution will ever have cause to regret their decision remains to be seen, but even if they did, a launch of this type would not be necessary today, though if it were it would probably be carried out with as little fuss. With powered life-boats and easier launching positions a boat could be launched with comparative speed, but the Lynmouth launch of 1899 serves as a splendid example of the feats of endurance which life-boatmen of the early days underwent as a part of their duty.

CHAPTER THREE

Whitby—1914

The possibility of using powered life-boats had been considered as far back as 1850, when various efforts were made to discover the suitability of building steam-driven boats, but at that time there were almost insuperable difficulties, and it was not until thirty-six years later that any definite move was made in this direction.

The main difficulties in using steam life-boats effectively at that time were threefold. Firstly, nine times out of ten the life-boat of those days had to be launched from a beach, and even if some practical way of launching a steam life-boat from a beach could be found there still remained the problem of keeping the fires for the boilers alight during the tremendous amount of tossing about the boat would receive near the shore. Secondly, such a life-boat would naturally be so heavy that the dangers of its capsizing on launching would be increased enormously. The third difficulty was one which troubled the Institution for many years. The only men available to crew the life-boats were fishermen who were only used to sails and oars, and to introduce steam life-boats would mean that each crew would have to be provided with a trained engineer to look after the boilers and all the mechanical parts of the boat. In those days no fisherman was competent to perform these duties. The same objection was raised on the introduction of motor life-boats, but here the objection was overcome as fishermen themselves turned to power-driven fishing boats and became used to maintaining marine engines. Even to this day a motor life-boat requires more care and attention than a pulling and sailing life-boat did, and this is why the motor mechanic of each life-boat crew receives a wage from the Institution and is employed on a full-time basis.

Also, if a steam life-boat were to replace an existing pulling and sailing life-boat, not only would an engineer have to be provided but it was quite likely that the former crew would refuse to serve in her. Tradition dies hard, and for fishermen to give up the type of boat they knew so well and trusted so much in exchange for the newness and uncertainty of steam would be unlikely.

Nevertheless in 1886 the Institution began to consider seriously the possibility of introducing steam life-boats to the service, and in 1888 the first steam life-boat was ordered. One of the technical difficulties which had caused considerable delay in the final design of the life-boat was that any vessel driven by a screw was liable to pick up drifting wreckage and ropes in its propeller, for it is amongst such wreckage that a life-boat spends the greater part of her working life. As we shall see, this is still a problem today, though there are several ways in which it can be overcome.

The first steam life-boat was not driven by a screw, but by a system of hydraulic jets. An inlet pipe was placed on either side of the boat amidships. Water was drawn in by a turbine and ejected at pressure through the pipes, so driving the boat along. Not only did this do away with the danger of fouling a propeller, but it also meant that the boat could be driven steadily. Screws at the stern of the vessel in the type of sea a life-boat has to meet would spend a large part of their time out of the water as the life-boat pitched, so losing a lot of power and causing the engines to race. This was avoided by placing the pipes amidships where they would not break the surface of the water.

In 1890 the steam life-boat *Duke of Northumberland* was stationed at Harwich. She had undergone exhaustive trials before the officials of the Institution were thoroughly satisfied with her. She was followed by the *City of Glasgow* in 1893 and by one or two others. Design of the later steam life-boats differed in several ways from the original.

But steam life-boats were never very successful, though some of them did excellent service. They had to lie at moorings and there were, and still are, very few places where this was possible. The weight of them meant that they needed a very deep draft, a grave disadvantage for a life-boat which very often has to work in shallow water, and the problem of finding engineers was a difficult one.

Altogether the Institution built six steam life-boats. Most life-boatmen were suspicious of them, and many preferred the old pulling and sailing boats. They had no objection to steam itself, for on many occasions a steam tug would tow a sailing life-boat as near as possible to the scene of a wreck, saving her crew from the dreadful task of pulling the boat through heavy seas. Usually a tug was most useful in pulling a life-boat out of a harbour mouth where wind and tide often combined to foil the life-boatmen's own efforts. The life-boatmen appreciated the help which steam power could give them, but felt that steam in the life-boat itself was not a great help. They were right.

Another reason for the rapid passing of the steam life-boat was that within a few years a more efficient means of power began to appear.

A petrol engine was fitted into a pulling and sailing life-boat for the first time in 1904, and so began a new era in the history of the Institution.

This new era was not altogether a happy one at the beginning. In the first place the problem of launching a motor life-boat was only slightly less acute than that of launching a steam life-boat—through the surf on a beach. Although the same problem of weight was not present, sea water could render the engine useless before the life-boat had really started. Therefore to begin with, the engine was regarded only as an auxiliary, and coxswains were instructed by the Institution to regard oars and sail as the main source of propulsion. In these early cases of fitting engines to already existing boats there was the problem of knowing where to place the engine so as to maintain the life-boat's very important balance. This was not easy in life-boats designed for pulling and sailing. There was the problem of racing screws when the propellers were lifted clear of the water. There was the very great danger of fire, for early petrol engines had an unhappy knack of bursting into flames at the slightest opportunity.

All this seemed to support many of the life-boat crews in the belief that pulling and sailing life-boats were still the best and most efficient means of saving lives at sea, and in fact it was not until 1908—four years after the introduction of an engine into a life-boat—that the first life-boat built with a motor was stationed at Stromness in Orkney.

The development of motor life-boats might well have been delayed for some considerable time had not something happened which, in the course of a few years, revolutionized mechanical transport of all types. On 4 August 1914 war broke out between Great Britain and Germany. The holocaust of the Great War had started.

In the course of the war many rescues were performed by the life-boat service which proved the efficiency of motor over pulling and sailing life-boats. One of the best examples of this was the wreck of the s.s. *Rohilla*.

The *Rohilla* was a 7,900-ton vessel owned by the British India Line. She had been taken over by the government at the outbreak of the war for use as a hospital ship, and she was on her way from Queensferry in the Firth of Forth to Dunkirk in France to bring back some of the men wounded in the trenches at the front. There were 229 people aboard her, including five nurses. On 30 October 1914 she ran aground on a dangerous reef of rocks at Saltwick Nab a mile or two south-east of Whitby in a ferocious east-south-easterly gale. The seas were so heavy that she broke in half almost immediately, and those in the after part of her were washed away and drowned. The fore part of the *Rohilla* lay helpless on the rocks, pounded by the mighty seas.

Distress signals were sent up as soon as she struck the rocks, and Coxswain Thomas Langlands of Whitby was called. But one glance told him that the sea was too rough to launch the Number One life-boat: no crew could row through the pounding surf and into the teeth of that gale to the wreck. Yet something would have to be done quickly, and the coxswain formed a plan. It was a desperate one but the situation called for desperate measures. He gave orders for the smaller Number Two life-boat to be taken from the harbour where she lay moored and transported by land to the cliff overlooking the wreck. This entailed a journey almost as difficult as the one undertaken at Lynmouth fifteen years before. The boat had to be manhandled over the eight-foot sea wall and along the rocks to the cliff where there might be calmer water to launch her. Scores of people helped to lift and drag the life-boat, and despite many declarations that the journey was impossible they managed to reach comparative shelter near the base of the cliffs. During the journey the boat was stove in in two places, but nevertheless she was launched, and the shore helpers stood and watched as the crew bent to their oars and pulled her through the foaming sea among the rocks to where the wreck lay a quarter of a mile from the shore. She reached the *Rohilla* and took off the five nurses and twelve of the men and brought them ashore. Then she went out again, the heavy seas pounding over her, and reached the wreck once more. This time they brought back eighteen men, but by now the boat was so severely damaged by her journey to the launching place and by the beating she had received against the rocks on her two journeys that she could not be launched again.

A member of the local life-boat committee then sent a message to Upgang a mile or two north of Whitby and asked for the Upgang boat to be brought to the same place and launched. In spite of the enormous difficulties of transporting the Upgang boat through Whitby this was done, the boat being dragged through the town by a team of horses and hundreds of helpers. She was lowered by ropes down the cliff face to the water. The crew waited until 2.30 when the tide had fallen and it was hoped that it might be possible to launch the boat and reach the wreck, but the sea showed no signs of abating and the coxswain and crew stood by until they could see a chance of getting away.

Meanwhile those on the shore were not idle. Telephone calls went out to the life-boat stations at Scarborough and Teesmouth asking for help, but the sea was running so high at Scarborough that the life-boat could not get clear of the harbour even with the assistance of a steam tug towing it. However, the weather seemed to moderate a little later, and at 3.30 the life-boat was towed out of the harbour by a steam trawler and reached the scene of the wreck at six o'clock. But it was now dark, and as it was wartime no lights could be shown, and there was nothing the life-boat could do until daylight, so she stood by until then.

At the same time the Teesmouth life-boat was alerted. This was a motor life-boat, but Teesmouth was some distance away from Whitby and when the call came it was realized that the life-boat could not get there in daylight. It was felt that it would be suicidal in the conditions to attempt to cross the harbour bar and proceed down the coast in darkness with no guiding lights, so the honorary secretary decided to wait until first light before sending the life-boat out.

At five o'clock in the morning she left her station, accompanied by the Tees Commissioners' tug, and crossing the bar she met tremendous seas. Dropping from the crest of a wave into the trough she sprang such a serious leak that the tug had to take the crew aboard and tow the life-boat to Middlesbrough.

At Whitby the Upgang crew were still standing by, and there was a slight chance that they might manage to reach the wreck at low water, so at nine o'clock the crew took their places and the life-boat was launched. But the sea was running so high and there was such a strong current between the Nab and the wreck that it was impossible. Time after time the crew bent to their oars, muscles cracking with the strain, but each time they were driven back. Once they managed to get within fifty yards of the *Rohilla* before being beaten back again, and eventually the crew were so exhausted that the attempt had to be given up.

When those on board the *Rohilla* saw the life-boat get so near them and fail, many of them, feeling that their last chance of rescue had gone, jumped overboard and tried to swim ashore. Seeing this, some of the people watching on the shore waded out into the seething water and managed to pull some of them to safety. But others were swept away and were never seen again.

Yet another attempt was made by the Whitby Number One life-boat, which was taken in tow by a trawler summoned by telegram from Hartlepool, but although they got within half a mile of the wreck the sea was still too heavy to approach any closer.

It was now obvious that no pulling life-boat could possibly reach the wreck in those conditions and the weather showed no sign of improving. The Teesmouth life-boat was out of commission and the next nearest motor life-boat was stationed at

Tynemouth 44 miles up the coast. This life-boat was summoned by telegram. The message was received at a quarter past four in the afternoon and Coxswain Robert Smith immediately set out in the life-boat for Whitby, despite having to sail down the unlit coast through that stormy night. He was enabled to do this by the fact that Captain H. E. Burton, the honorary superintendent of the life-boat, sailed with her and, thanks to the fact that Captain Burton knew the whole coastline intimately, they reached Whitby safely at one o'clock in the morning and put into the harbour.

Preparations were made to rescue those who were still on the *Rohilla* after two days' exposure to wind and weather. Oil was taken on board the life-boat and the Whitby second coxswain went aboard to act as pilot, for Coxswain Smith was unfamiliar with the tides and rocks round Saltwick Nab. The gale showed no sign of slackening, but at half-past six in the morning the life-boat crept out of Whitby harbour and headed for the wreck. She approached within two hundred yards of the *Rohilla* and then turned seawards, and the watchers on the shore felt their hearts sinking. What was wrong with this great motor life-boat? It looked as though she was already admitting defeat and was turning for home. But when she got beyond the wreck she stopped, and the oil she had taken on board was discharged over the boiling sea. It seemed to those watching that this was a waste of time, that no amount of oil could possibly calm those waters, but the oil spread and the tide carried it towards the wreck; and as they watched, the people on the cliff saw the sea round the *Rohilla* slacken and drop and change from the terrible foam-flecked, churning waves into a yeasty, oily, gently heaving mass. It seemed like a miracle.

But there was no time to be lost. The effects of the oil would soon pass as the rapid current carried it away again. The lifeboat turned and raced round the wreck to her lee side, swung for a sickening minute broadside on to the waves and moved in to the side of the *Rohilla*. Ropes were let down from the *Rohilla*'s deck to the life-boat, and men began to swarm down them into the little boat alongside. But the sea had not yet finished and was not to be so easily baulked. Two tremendous waves bore down on the wreck and swamped her, one after the other, but the life-boat simply disappeared under the spray and re-appeared each time, still upright, and within a quarter of an hour fifty men had been taken off. The last one to leave the *Rohilla* was the captain.

Then as the life-boat drew away from the wreck and left the shelter of her side another huge wave bore down on her and struck her broadside on. It seemed she must capsize with the weight of so many men aboard her, but she righted herself and the coxswain brought her under control. In a short time the life-boat entered Whitby harbour and it seemed the whole population of the town was there to welcome her. The rescued men had been exposed on the deck of the *Rohilla* for two days in that fearsome weather. Many of them were dressed only in pyjamas and some of them were barefoot.

The R.N.L.I. awarded three gold medals and two silver medals as well as other awards for this rescue. Coxswain Thomas Langlands of Whitby, Coxswain Robert Smith and Captain Burton of Tynemouth were awarded gold medals, and Second Coxswain Richard Eglon of Whitby and Second Coxswain James Brownlee of Tynemouth were awarded the silver medal.

And if ever proof was needed that motor life-boats could perform rescues impossible to pulling and sailing life-boats the rescue by the Tynemouth life-boat at Whitby provided it.

CHAPTER FOUR

Runswick—1934

The Great War was called the Petrol War, for during it tremendous advances were made in all the mechanical fields. This had to be in order to contend with the German menace. Motor transport really came into its own, tanks were used for the first time and aircraft developed at an amazing speed, for the first flight had only taken place eleven years before the war began. In this progress the life-boat service was for the time being unable to compete. All available resources were being used to supply the men fighting at the front and the R.N.L.I. could not be regarded as a fighting service, although the rescues performed by the life-boat stations round our coast were in many cases as dangerous and arduous as the life of the men in the trenches. But the service had no priority. Life-boats were already in existence and these life-boats would have to serve their turn in the meantime, although it very soon became obvious that pulling and sailing life-boats were rapidly becoming out of date.

Therefore once the war was over in November 1918 plans were put forward for converting the entire fleet of life-boats to motor power. This was an enormous undertaking. At that time there were over 250 life-boat stations in the British Isles, and it was a question not only of providing new boats but also of building suitable places for these new boats to be launched. Many of the old stations could of course be closed down, for the motor life-boat even in its early days had a far wider range of operation than a pulling and sailing boat.

The work was started, but it proceeded slowly. Not only was a lot of work needed to find out the requirements of the different stations, but it involved an enormous expenditure. New boat-houses were built. Slipways were erected from boathouses standing at pier heads and on cliff sides so that the life-boat

could run straight into the water. At the same time came tractors which could tow the life-boat from its boathouse over a
beach and push it into the water in the way that teams of
horses had done in the old days. The organization of this
change-over took a long time. The last occasion when horses
were used to launch a life-boat was in 1934, and in fact the last
pulling and sailing life-boat, stationed at New Quay in Car-
diganshire, was not withdrawn from service until 1948.

The early motor life-boats had single engines and an auxiliary
sail, for it sometimes happened that the engine failed when at
sea, and a sail was essential or the life-boat was left helpless.
One of the most comforting features to the life-boatmen was the
fact that these new boats had shelter in them. The engine and
the controls had to be covered and this cover soon extended to
protect the crew as well. Later, twin engines were introduced and
this lessened the necessity for having a sail, as the chances of
both engines failing were far less likely, and even with only one
engine working the life-boat could still be manœuvred reasonably well.

The old problem of wreckage fouling the propellers was overcome to a certain extent by placing the life-boat's screws in
tunnels well forward of the stern. This lessened the speed of the
life-boat a little, but sailing in the conditions a life-boat is
usually out in, speed is of minor importance. The tunnels protected the screws from floating wreckage, although there was
still and always would be a chance that some wreckage would
be drawn in. Furthermore the placing of the screws forward did
away with the other difficulty of the propellers racing when the
life-boat lifted her stern clear of the water, so steady propulsion
was possible.

The introduction of motor life-boats increased the efficiency
of the service enormously, and it also meant that many stations
could be closed down and the cost of the changeover was offset
by the saving in cost of maintaining these stations. This did not
mean that life-boat stations in small isolated places round the
coast disappeared. Many of the Institution's stations are placed
in tiny fishing villages far from the noise and bustle of big ports
and harbours. One of them is situated where there is no village
at all. This is the Humber life-boat station, right at the tip of

Spurn Point, and this station is so isolated that there are no means for the crew to earn a living. It is almost completely cut off from the world, but it guards the important entry to the river Humber for shipping going to Grimsby and Hull, and because of its isolation the Institution keeps a full-time crew here, the only station where the men are all paid a wage.

The story of Coxswain Robert Cross of the Humber is typical of the selflessness and the single-minded purpose of the men who form the life-boat crews.

Robert Cross joined the crew of the Humber life-boat in 1902 and served with it for six years. Then he bought a share in a herring drifter and this occupied his time sufficiently for him to leave the station temporarily. But the call of the service must still have been with him, for in 1909 he went out with the Flamborough life-boat to the rescue of some fishing cobles. A gale had sprung up and the cobles were in urgent need of help. Despite the efforts of the life-boat two of the cobles were lost, and Robert Cross lost his brother and his brother's two sons in one day. This personal disaster seems to have made him more determined than ever to devote his life to saving others from shipwreck, for he returned to the Humber in 1911 and became coxswain of the life-boat. He remained at the station for thirty-one years before he retired at the age of sixty-seven, and in that time he helped to save 453 lives. He was awarded the George Medal, and during the second world war was twice awarded the Institution's gold medal.

The heroic stories of the life-boat service are all the more impressive because they are done quietly and rarely receive much publicity in the press, or if they do, it is hard for the readers to understand fully the ordeals which many of the life-boatmen go through. Life-boatmen have never considered their own safety when the safety of others is in peril, and on many occasions coxswains have taken incredible risks in performing their duties. These risks are always calculated, for the coxswains know exactly what they are facing, but this does not prevent them from attempting them.

Usually, thanks to superb seamanship, the attempts are successful, but sometimes disasters happen in spite of all they can do.

Perhaps one of the most heroic acts in the history of the life-boat service and one of the most noble acts of self-sacrifice happened in 1934 at Runswick in Yorkshire.

Coxswain Robert Patton was born in 1887 and he joined the crew of the Runswick life-boat at the age of sixteen. There was a tradition of life-boat service in this family of fishermen. His father had been second coxswain for twenty-seven years, and his brother became coxswain in 1946. Robert Patton was one of eighteen men who received special rewards for their part in the service to the *Rohilla* at Whitby in 1914. He became coxswain in 1931. He was known locally as a fine man, an excellent fisherman and a first-rate life-boat coxswain.

At four o'clock in the morning of 8 February 1934 the coastguard at Staithes saw distress signals being fired about five miles north-north-west of Staithes Nab. There was a strong gale blowing, the sea was heavy and it was raining.

The coastguard rang the life-boat station at Runswick, and at 4.25 *The Always Ready* was launched. She cleared the shelter of Runswick Bay and punched her way through the seas northwards. At half-past five she reached the scene of the accident. There were two vessels there, one a salvage steamer from West Hartlepool called the *Disperser* which had been in tow of a tug. The *Disperser* was sinking and by the time the life-boat reached her seven members of her crew of eight had been taken off by the tug. But there was still one man left on board, and he was lame.

With great difficulty Coxswain Patton manœvred the life-boat alongside the sinking steamer. The crew could see the lone man on the deck and they called on him to jump. It was a time for quick action and careful judgment, for holding the life-boat alongside the steamer in those seas was a difficult and dangerous business. Instead of jumping the man lowered himself over the side and hung there. Coxswain Patton shouted to him to jump, but it seemed as though the man had suddenly lost his nerve, for instead of letting go and dropping safely into the life-boat he clung on tighter than ever as though frozen against the side of the wallowing steamer.

Coxswain Patton grabbed hold of him and shouted to him to

let go, but the man still held tightly to the deck rails as though terrified to release his grip.

At that moment the sea began to carry the life-boat away from the steamer's side, and Coxswain Patton found himself in an appalling quandary. He could let go of the man, in which case he would almost certainly fall into the sea and be drowned, for he had no life-belt, or he could hold on and let himself be dragged into the water with him. He made the decision in a split second and held on to the man.

The life-boat was swept away and Coxswain Patton found himself being dragged over the side into the water, still clinging to the man who was himself still clinging to the side of the steamer.

And at that moment the sea played a terrible trick. It flung the life-boat back at the steamer as though it were throwing a rubber ball against a wall, and Coxswain Patton took the full force and weight of the life-boat against his life-belt.

The crew quickly pulled the man aboard, but to drag a man over the projecting side of the life-boat took time, and before they could pull out their coxswain he had been crushed twice more between the life-boat and the steamer. At last they got him aboard the life-boat and laid him gently on the deck.

A minute or two later the steamer sank, and the life-boat turned for home. She reached Runswick at a quarter past six, and Coxswain Patton was rushed to hospital. An examination showed that amongst a host of terrible injuries the worst were several broken ribs, a fractured vertebrae and his pelvis was fractured in three places.

Two days later he was conscious and able to speak to an official of the Institution. He had been fully aware of the risk he had run, but the man had been lame and had no life-belt.

'I could not let the poor lad go, as he might have drowned,' he said simply.

A week later Coxswain Robert Patton died from the injuries he had received, and he was posthumously awarded the gold medal. To commemorate his act of self-sacrifice the name of the life-boat was changed to *Robert Patton—The Always Ready*.

The wrecked St Ives life-boat stranded on the rocks at Godrevy Head. Only one member of the crew of eight survived. See chapter VI

Coxswain Henry Blogg of Cromer, the greatest coxswain of all time. See chapter IX

Coxswain Thomas Cocking who lost his life in the St Ives life-boat disaster in January 1939. See chapter VI

CHAPTER FIVE

Ballycotton—1936

Life-boats did not appear in Ireland until some time after the
first life-boats appeared in England, Scotland and Wales. Indeed, there seems to have been very little done to provide a
service in Ireland until shortly after the formation of the Shipwreck Institution. Then two years after the formation of the
Institution—in 1826—a 30-foot life-boat was sent to Arklow in
County Wicklow, and from then on more and more boats were
sent to key points round the Irish coast.

The story of the life-boat service in Ireland is a happy one,
because in spite of all the political upheavals in that country
through the first forty years of this century, the R.N.L.I. continued to operate the service with the greatest possible co-
operation from all concerned. In 1920, at the height of the Irish
troubles, a Roman Catholic priest and a Protestant archbishop
both took part in the dedication of a new life-boat at Kings-
town, and the ceremony seems to have been like a breath of
fresh air in the middle of the turbulence and heartbreak of civil
war.

At the time of partition, when the Irish Free State and
Northern Ireland became separate, the Governor-General of
the Free State became patron of the Northern Ireland life-boat
area and the Governor of Northern Ireland became patron of
the Free State area, an example of mutual co-operation unusual in those times.

Today in the Republic of Ireland the Royal National Life-
boat Institution's flag flies over the Irish life-boathouses and the
administration is carried out from the London headquarters.

Although not so old in history as other life-boat stations the
Irish life-boats have performed services as dangerous and as exhausting as any others.

Some rescues are performed in a matter of minutes. Some

may take hours. All can be equally dangerous. The service which must stand out as one of the longest and most dangerous was performed by the Ballycotton life-boat between 11 and 14 February 1936.

Ballycotton lies on the southern shore of Ireland, some miles west of Cork, and overlooking the busy shipping lanes round that coast. Out at sea nearby stands the Daunt lightship, guarding the dangerous Daunt Rock.

On 7 February a south-easterly gale sprang up round the south coast of Ireland, which increased to such an extent that by the 10th it was blowing at hurricane force. Even in the shelter of the harbour the waves were enormous, and Coxswain Patrick Sliney and his crew ran ropes from the life-boat *Mary Stanford* to prevent her being dashed against the breakwater. During the night of the 10th the coxswain's own motor boat broke adrift and he and several men spent the whole night trying to reach her and bring her under control. They were fishermen, these Ballycotton men, and the boat meant his livelihood to Patrick Sliney. At seven o'clock in the morning they had succeeded in securing the motor boat, and it was at that moment, when they were tired with their night's work, that the call came.

The wind was ferocious, uprooting trees, bringing down the telephone wires and even lifting great blocks of stone out of the quay, some of them weighing as much as a ton, and whirling them away as if they had been pebbles.

Mr Robert Mahony, the Ballycotton postmaster and honorary secretary of the life-boat station, received a message to say that the Daunt Rock lightship had broken loose and was drifting. The message was brought to Ballycotton by hand as all the telephone wires were down.

The honorary secretary told the coxswain, who had just returned from securing his boat. After he had given the message neither of the men spoke. They saw the weather and they knew the dangers. They also knew that a drifting lightship was a double peril. Not only was it a danger to shipping as a drifting vessel, but also the fact that she was a lightship out of position could cause vessels to proceed on the wrong course. The seas were breaking clean over the life-boathouse where the boarding boat was kept. Without a word, Coxswain Sliney turned and walked down to the harbour.

A little later the honorary secretary followed and was amazed to see the life-boat already slipping out between the piers of the harbour. The coxswain had quietly collected his crew and had not fired the maroons so as not to alarm the village.

Mr Mahony watched as the 51-foot life-boat reached the open sea and began to dance in a mad jig to the tune of the waves. People from the village gathered in silence to watch her go, and then slowly and quietly made their way to the church to pray. . . .

To the west of Ballycotton lie two islands, and on the seaward one stands a lighthouse. The lantern of the lighthouse was 196 feet high and the spray from the sea was flying over it. Coxswain Sliney took the life-boat between the islands and once clear of them met mountainous seas. She dropped from the first crest into the following trough with such a sickening thud that the crew were certain the engines must tear their way through the bottom of the boat. But they were still in place, and the crew were reassured. If the engines remained fixed after that they would withstand anything.

Now the life-boat was running before the sea, which was so rough and confused that the coxswain decided to put out his drogue. This is a cone-shaped canvas bag with a fixed mouth and is towed behind a boat to retard its progress and steady it, but as the drogue was being put out, Coxswain Sliney had to ease the engines, and a heavy sea swept into the cockpit of the life-boat, knocking the crew all over the place. When they picked themselves up they found that the drogue ropes had fouled but that the drogue was drawing.

Visibility was so bad that the coxswain could see nothing of the shore and found no sign of the drifting lightship, so he decided to make for the lightship's normal position in the hope of picking her up. He turned and headed into the sea for about seven miles, but his course under those conditions was so erratic and the visibility so poor that he could not be sure when he reached the lightship's position. So he set a course for the big port of Queenstown to try to get the latest information.

He reached Queenstown at eleven in the morning and he had to spray oil on the water to calm the sea sufficiently at the harbour mouth to allow him to enter. He got the lightship's exact position, tried to telephone his honorary secretary but found the lines were still down, and immediately put to sea again.

They found the Daunt Rock lightship at midday about a quarter of a mile away from the rock and half a mile from the shore. She was riding to a single anchor. Two vessels were standing by her, one of which left when the life-boat arrived. The other, the destroyer *Tenedos*, remained to give what help she could.

Coxswain Sliney managed to speak to the crew of the lightship through his loud-hailer. The crew did not want to leave their vessel, for they knew the dangers to shipping of a lightship out of position, but they were afraid that their only anchor might not hold in those seas and they asked the life-boat to stand by. The coxswain agreed to do so, but conditions were too bad for him to anchor, so the life-boat spent the night steaming and drifting up and down near the lightship while the wind lashed the crew and the sea soaked them to the skin.

At half-past three the following afternoon the wind had moderated slightly and the *Tenedos* attempted to pass a line to the lightship in the hope of being able to draw a wire hawser over to her and take her in tow, but all attempts failed. Even with the life-boat's help the rope kept parting, and on the one occasion they did manage to get a wire hawser aboard the strength of the sea was such that the hawser snapped.

By now the crew of the life-boat were soaked and exhausted. They had had no food for over twenty-four hours, and as the *Tenedos* was going to stand by all night they turned for Queenstown once more. They arrived at 9.30 in the evening. This time the coxswain managed to telephone Mr Mahony at Ballycotton, and Mr Mahony immediately set out for Queenstown by car with spare equipment and dry clothing for the crew. It was a difficult journey, for trees brought down by the gale were still strewn across the roads.

During the night some of the crew managed to snatch a few hours' sleep, but early the following morning the life-boat set out again for the lightship. The *Tenedos* left and the lightship asked the life-boat to stand by. This she did. During the day the wind went down still further but the sea remained very rough. She stayed by the lightship all night again, and in the morning returned once more to Queenstown for petrol as her supply was getting very low. The life-boat was refuelled at Queenstown and left again at four in the afternoon. She reached the lightship at dusk and found the Irish Lights vessel *Isolda* standing by. The captain of the *Isolda* told the coxswain that he would stand by all night and try to take the lightship in tow in the morning, but the weather was worsening once more.

The lightship was showing a red light fore and aft as a sign that she was out of position, and at eight o'clock a heavy sea swept over the vessel, carrying away the forward light. And now the wind was shifting and the lightship was drifting nearer the Daunt Rock, the very rock it was her duty to warn shipping off. If the wind shifted much further she must drive on to the rock. The *Isolda* was powerless to help, but it was obvious now that, despite the dreadful conditions, the crew of the lightship must be taken off.

The coxswain weighed up the chances and worked out what he would have to do. He hailed the crew of the lightship and told them what he intended. The lightship by now was acting like a frightened horse, bucking and leaping against the anchor rope, rolling madly from side to side as though desperate to tear itself loose.

The coxswain took the life-boat ahead of the lightship and pumped oil to try and calm the water, but the tide was so strong that the effect was soon lost. Then he went astern of her and, shouting to the mechanic to put both engines full ahead, he steered alongside. As he came up to the heaving vessel both engines were flung into reverse, and for a second the life-boat stood still alongside the lightship. In that second's pause one member of the crew jumped aboard. Four more times Coxswain Sliney executed the same tricky manœuvre, and now six members of the lightship's crew were safely aboard, but the fourth time the lightship heeled violently over the life-boat and crashed on top of her, tearing away the rail and damaging the fender and the deck.

Coxswain Sliney went in again, but no one jumped. There were still two members of the crew clinging to the rails, but they seemed to have lost their nerve and could not make that frightening leap backwards into the life-boat. At the risk of having them swept overboard the coxswain sent some members of his crew forward and when he came alongside for the sixth and last time, they grabbed the two men and pulled them aboard.

At eleven o'clock on the night of 13 February, the life-boat returned to Queenstown with the eight members of the light-ship's crew. Soon after leaving the lightship one of the rescued men became hysterical because of the ordeal he had been through, and he had to be held down forcibly by two members of the life-boat's crew who were themselves exhausted. At a quarter to one the following afternoon the life-boat returned to her station at Ballycotton, having been out on service for 76½ hours. The coxswain had a poisoned arm and all the crew were suffering from colds and salt-water burns and they were in the last stages of exhaustion. And yet after all that time at sea the coxswain and his crew had performed a feat of seamanship in appalling conditions which even in fresh and alert men would have been a difficult one.

The coxswain received the gold medal for this service, the second coxswain and the motor mechanic received the silver medal, and the four members of the crew received the bronze.

And it may be of interest to record the names of the members of that crew: Coxswain Patrick Sliney; Second Coxswain John L. Walsh; Motor Mechanic Thomas Sliney; Michael C. Walsh; Thomas F. Walsh; John S. Sliney and William Sliney. A crew of seven and only two surnames among them—another proof that the manning of many of our life-boats truly runs in families.

Patrick Sliney no longer serves with the Ballycotton life-boat. His days for that sort of work are past. He is a little troubled by deafness, an affliction which first appeared shortly after the Daunt Rock lightship service, and which was probably caused by the experience he had during those hectic three days.

CHAPTER SIX

St Ives—1939

Until recently the problem of self-righting life-boats as opposed to ordinary ones caused the Institution a great deal of discord, not only amongst its designers and engineers but also amongst those who man the life-boats. From the very earliest days the principle of a self-righting life-boat was considered a practical proposition. In fact Wouldhave's original model was based on this principle. The difficulty was to design a boat which would right itself after capsizing without sacrificing any of the stability which a life-boat must have.

Many of the early pulling and sailing life-boats were self-righters, and it is interesting to trace the development of this type of boat.

The first suggestion of the self-righting principle seems to be contained in the life-boat designed by George Palmer. Palmer lived in Essex and was very active in the affairs of the Institution. He became connected with it in 1826 and served for many years as its deputy chairman. Before that, however, he had designed a life-boat which had been adopted by the Institution. She was sharp-ended and had a rounded section and looked very like a whale-boat. She had three air cases on either side, another in the bows and two in the stern, and she had four tin gunwale cases built high to prevent her from capsizing. Her design was such that she could heel over and dip her mast in the water but would still return to an upright position. Palmer's design was as far as self-righting went at that time. This type of boat was introduced into the service in 1828 and did not finally go out of favour until 1852.

The Institution itself went through a bad time from 1828 until 1849, and its work seems almost to have come to a standstill. There was no strong hand to guide its affairs and things became unco-ordinated. The Prime Minister, the Earl of Liverpool,

President of the Shipwreck Institution, died in 1828, and no new President was appointed.

Now it often happens that a spectacular disaster suddenly stimulates the public mind and brings things to their attention in a way that might otherwise never happen. We have seen how the wreck of the *Adventurer* caused the Gentlemen of the Lawe House to hold a competition for a life-boat from which Wouldhave's design and Greathead's *Original* emerged. It is a strange coincidence that another wreck at exactly the same place should start the upward climb of the Institution's fortunes once again.

On 4 December 1849 the brig *Betsy* was wrecked at the entrance to the Tyne, and the South Shields life-boat, manned by twenty-four men, went out to her. The life-boat capsized. In fact she was thrown by the sea stem over stern and turned a complete somersault. Only four of the life-boatmen survived.

This disaster caused a tremendous outcry, as had Grace Darling's rescue of the *Forfarshire* survivors eleven years before, but this time the fact that it was one of the Institution's life-boats which suffered made the benefit more direct. People began to realize once more the supreme importance of an efficient life-boat service. Queen Victoria and Prince Albert took a personal interest in the Institution's affairs, but what was far more important was the fact that the fourth Duke of Northumberland became the Institution's second President. He became President in 1851, twenty-three years after the death of the previous one. The Duke of Northumberland was himself an admiral who had served under Collingwood who had led the fleet to battle at Trafalgar under Nelson and who had assumed command after Nelson's death. The 'Sailor Duke' later became First Lord of the Admiralty.

The effect of his presence was immediate. He offered a prize of a hundred guineas for a new life-boat design, and appointed a committee of experts to scrutinize the models submitted. In a circular introducing the competition the Duke referred to the disaster at South Shields and enumerated the bad points of the life-boats then in service which he hoped would be eliminated in the designs submitted. It is worth detailing these points as they were set out in the Duke's pamphlet:

1. That they do not right themselves in the event of being upset.

2. That they are too heavy to be readily launched and transported along the coast in case of need.
3. That they do not free themselves of water fast enough.
4. That they are very expensive.

The response to the competition was most gratifying and in some cases most amusing. Amongst several extraordinary designs submitted was a life-boat of 'whimsical construction' which was open to the sea at the bottom. Another, also open at the bottom, was equipped with 222 gallons of fresh water and a kettle guaranteed to boil in ten minutes. And there was a design for a life-boat built of wickerwork and covered in canvas which could be rolled along the beach and then opened out when it had to be launched.

Altogether 280 models were submitted, and from these the committee of experts selected thirty-seven for more detailed examination. As a result of this the prize was eventually awarded to James Beeching of Great Yarmouth, who in fact had built a life-boat to his own design before the result of the competition was announced.

She was thirty-six feet long, pulled twelve oars, had a lug foresail and mizzen and weighed two and a half tons. If the boat turned over there was two and a quarter tons of water ballast and an iron keel to drag her upright again, and there were raised air cases at stem and stern for buoyancy.

On trial she outshone even what was predicted for her, and she was stationed at Ramsgate.

Although she was so successful the Institution itself had Beeching's design modified by James Peake, a shipwright at Woolwich Dockyard. Peake made the boat smaller than Beeching's original design, and life-boats were built with his modifications.

So appeared the first self-righting life-boats, and the principle of self-righting might have been accepted there and then but for the fact that Beeching himself, in subsequent designs, made alterations of his own. He converted the end air cases into storage lockers so that they were no longer airtight, and this may have been one of the causes of an accident to two self-righting life-boats which together made the biggest disaster the Institution has ever known.

On 9 December 1886 the German barque *Mexico* of Hamburg, which was bound for Guayaquil in Ecuador from Liverpool, went aground in a gale near Southport. Distress signals were seen at Southport life-boat station at nine o'clock that evening and preparations were made to launch. The horses dragged the life-boat for three and a half miles along the shore before she could be launched, but eventually, with a crew of fifteen, she got away successfully.

She reached the *Mexico* at one o'clock in the morning, and making to windward of her the coxswain prepared to drop the anchor and veer down on the cable to the barque. As he was about to do so a heavy sea struck the life-boat and she capsized. Two hours later the life-boat came ashore three miles from Southport. There were two men in her—the other thirteen had been swept away and drowned.

A quarter of an hour before the Southport life-boat set out from her boathouse the St Anne's life-boat was asked to stand by. She had a crew of fourteen. She was launched at 10.30, and those watching on the shore saw the crew row the first five hundred yards before they hoisted sail, and the life-boat moved into the darkness of the open sea. It was the last time her crew were seen alive. No one knows for certain what happened to her. Watchers at the boathouse at Southport saw two red lights burning out at sea later that evening, and these may have been signals from the life-boat.

At a quarter-past eleven the following morning she was found washed up on the shore, bottom up, with three of her crew hanging on the thwarts head downwards. It has been argued that one of the causes of this disaster was the fact that the coxswain was consumptive and should never have been in charge of the life-boat on such a service.

The Lytham life-boat, which had arrived at her station only a fortnight earlier, was launched at ten o'clock on her first service. She was rowed down the river Ribble, then hoisted sail in the open sea. She was filled with water several times, but managed to free herself. She came within a quarter of a mile of the wreck and the crew lowered the sail and unstepped the mast. She was struck again by the sea with such force that three of her oars were broken. But the coxswain anchored her and veered down alongside the *Mexico*, which by now was almost on her beam ends. The crew had lashed themselves to the rigging to prevent being washed overboard, and the life-boat succeeded in taking the twelve of them off.

The loss of two life-boats and twenty-seven men gave the self-righting principle a jolt from which it is only now recovering fully. Some people contend that a self-righting life-boat was too narrow in the beam and could capsize more easily. A broader beamed life-boat might not right itself if it capsized, but the chances of its capsizing in the first place were considerably less. Many examples have been held up to illustrate the correctness of both these theories, and it is only since 1958 that the design of the Oakley self-righter seems to have answered all the problems satisfactorily, though even now the controversy is not dead.

The Oakley life-boat is almost as broad in the beam as any other in the life-boat service, so it is as little likely to capsize as they are. However, if it does there is a system whereby one and a half tons of water ballast is quickly transferred into a tank on the port side of the boat if it heels over to an angle of over 110°, and this serves to swing the life-boat upright again.

But there was one very potent argument in favour of those who distrusted self-righting boats. Granted a life-boat might right itself after capsizing—but what happened if the crew were thrown out of her?

At the beginning of 1939 the shadow of war was already looming over Great Britain, but in the first month of the year a heavier shadow was cast over the little Cornish seaside resort of St Ives.

It was at two o'clock in the morning of 23 January that the honorary secretary received a telephone call from the coastguard to say that an unidentified vessel was in a dangerous position two miles away from Cape Cornwall. That vessel is still unidentified today although it seems almost certain that she must have been the s.s. *Wilston* of Glasgow. She had left Newport in Monmouthshire a day and a half before with a crew of thirty. Somewhere she sank with the loss of her entire crew. Wreckage and bodies washed ashore near Cape Cornwall two days later were identified as coming from the *Wilston*.

A very strong west-north-westerly gale was blowing and the sea was exceptionally heavy. If the St Ives life-boat was to be launched she would have to travel eleven miles round the coast to the vessel in distress, and she would be sailing directly into the gale almost the whole way. The coxswain was willing to go, but before the final decision was made the coastguard contacted the life-boat station at Sennen Cove just north of Land's End to see if assistance could be given from there. Sennen Cove was nearer and the gale would not prove so difficult for her. Everything seemed to indicate that a launch from Sennen Cove would be quicker, safer and have a better chance of success than a launch from St Ives.

There was only one drawback. Such was the position of the life-boat station at Sennen Cove that the life-boat could not be launched for two hours on either side of low tide, and when the message came through the tide was low. Sennen Cove was helpless.

When this news reached St Ives life-boat station Coxswain Thomas Cocking immediately prepared to launch. He fired the maroons and the crew gathered at the boathouse. One member of the crew was ill. He was nevertheless preparing to go out, but William Freeman, a 36-year-old fisherman who had never been out with the life-boat before, volunteered to take his place.

Launching at St Ives is difficult. The life-boat is towed from the boathouse by a tractor, along the front, through a gap in the wall and so into the harbour. When the tide is out the tractor has to push the life-boat over a wide stretch of sand before it reaches the water.

At half past two in the morning the life-boat was successfully launched. Such was the state of the wind and sea that over eighty helpers were needed on the shore to get her into the water. The life-boat herself was a reserve boat from Padstow called *John and Sarah Eliza Stych*, a 35½-foot self-righter with a single petrol engine and an auxiliary sail. She was on duty at St Ives because almost exactly a year earlier the St Ives life-boat had been wrecked while rescuing the crew of the Hungarian ship *Alba*. The life-boat crew and all those she had rescued were brought safely ashore, but the life-boat herself became a total loss, and at the beginning of 1939 a new boat had not yet arrived.

The life-boat was soon swallowed in the darkness of that wild night, and those on shore waited patiently for news of her. Her chances of reaching the vessel seemed remote in those conditions, and at that time there was no radio-telephone or wireless. Once the life-boat was launched communication with the shore was limited to visual signals, and at 4.20 in the morning, signals from the life-boat were seen only a mile or two away. They were red flares which meant *more help needed*.

This was an ominous message, especially in view of the fact that by that time the life-boat should have been well on her way to the casualty, and the life-saving team was ordered out. The Penlee life-boat, thirty miles away round the peninsula, was summoned to help and she was launched at five o'clock.

Meanwhile those on shore could only wait and hope and wonder. Scores of people gathered in the chill darkness, waiting silently for news that never seemed to come. What had happened to the St Ives life-boat?

St Ives lies at the west side of the deep bowl of St Ives Bay. The bay is sheltered, but beyond St Ives Head the life-boat met terrifying seas sweeping down on her from the westward, steep and powerful, whipped to a frenzy by the roaring wind, and it was into this solid mass of water that the life-boat had to battle her way, a small, frail speck in the vastness of the waves. She stood well out to sea to keep clear of the land, for the tide was now flooding and she could be hurled in amongst the rocks as though she was a featherweight. Up the enormous walls of water she rode and plunged sickeningly down the other side, the coxswain fighting to keep her bow head to sea. If she sheered slightly either to port or starboard the sea would swamp her. Coxswain Cocking fought the power of the elements with every ounce of strength and energy he possessed, but it was not enough. She reached the crest of one wave and began her plunge into the trough, and as she did so she sheered to one side.

That was the start of disaster.

Before she could be brought round to face the next sea it struck her on the starboard bow with such force that she capsized. She righted herself within seconds and came up again, but her crew had been halved. In that appalling welter of confusion the coxswain, the bowman, the signalman and one of the crew had been washed overboard. The assistant motor mechanic, John Cocking, was the son of the coxswain who was lost. William Barber, the bowman, had gone, leaving his brother Matthew, who was acting as second coxswain, behind in the life-boat. There were four men left in her. Four men left to handle her when before eight had hardly been able to do so.

William Freeman was washed partly overboard when the life-boat capsized, but he managed to keep hold of the gunwale and two other members of the crew dragged him back on board again. They heard a shout from the water but saw nothing, and the life-boat's engine had stalled, as it was designed to do when the boat capsized, so they could not start a search immediately. While Motor Mechanic Richard Stevens prepared to restart the engine the others cut away some of the life-boat's gear which had been partly washed out of her, as they were afraid it might foul their propeller. In a few minutes the single engine was restarted. The motor mechanic engaged gear and the engine stalled. He started the engine again and engaged gear again, and again it stalled. Despite their efforts to cut the gear away a rope must have fouled the propeller. He started the engine again and engaged astern gear, in the hope that the propeller blades would chop through the rope. It was useless. The engine stalled again.

The life-boat was helpless. They could no longer keep her head to the sea, and the boat was being thrown around by the immense waves. They dropped their anchor and veered out the cable to try to hold her steady, and then they tried to step the mizzen mast so that with her sail they might be able to control the life-boat while her anchor held her reasonably steady meantime. But with only four men left on board this task was impossible.

It was then that they burnt the red flares asking urgently for help. They saw the coastguard's answering flares, but each of them knew that the chances of help reaching them in time were remote. If their anchor held they might possibly ride out the storm. It was their only hope. It was a new rope, never used before, but the strain of holding the life-boat in those seas was too great and it soon parted.

Now the life-boat was truly at the mercy of the pitiless elements. The force of wind and sea began to propel her across the mouth of St Ives Bay towards Godrevy Head on the east side. All this time the mechanic was working desperately at the engine. It was functioning perfectly, but each time he tried to engage gear it stalled. The life-boat was swinging wildly in the seas, and if one struck her at the wrong time the crew knew very well what would happen. Half way across St Ives Bay another sea hit her when she was beam on to it, and the life-boat capsized again. William Freeman was under the canopy where the engine was controlled from, and he managed to hold on to the starting handle. The pressure of air trapped under the canopy kept the water out, and even when Freeman was upside down with the keel of the boat above him he was not under water. When the life-boat righted herself Motor Mechanic Stevens was missing.

Three men were left aboard the life-boat drifting helplessly nearer and nearer the rocks on Godrevy Head. They huddled together aft, appalled by what had happened. One man had lost his father, another his brother. They were helpless, but before they had time to gather their thoughts Matthew Barber suddenly shouted:

'Look out—a big sea coming!'

He had scarcely spoken when the sea struck for a third time and the life-boat capsized yet again. When she righted herself William Freeman found himself alone. He felt the others being washed past him, but he was powerless to help and he never saw them go.

Three minutes later the life-boat struck the rocks stern first. She was flung on to a ledge and, as the sea spewed her up and receded for a time as though satisfied with its work, the sole survivor crawled out and, still crawling, began to drag himself away. A sea overtook him as though anxious that nothing should be left, but it did not draw him back.

Shaken and confused, he managed to reach a nearby farm-house. The farmer and his wife took him in and put him to bed. He was badly cut and bruised. Then the farmer cycled into Hayle, telephoned for a doctor, and then rang the coastguard at St Ives.

And so, shortly after seven o'clock in the morning, news

reached St Ives that her life-boat was wrecked and only one member of her crew was left alive.

It was a disaster of the first magnitude. Flags flew at half mast in St Ives, all public entertainments were cancelled. The whole village virtually went into mourning. The life-boat was found on Godrevy Head. The engine was still in working order, and although the propeller blades were dented, there was nothing found fouling it. The engine was removed and the remains of the life-boat were burnt in the same way as the last life-boat had been burnt a year earlier to prevent souvenir hunters taking pieces away.

By a cynical coincidence the Hungarian Embassy in London had been informed that same day by the Hungarian Government of awards which were to be made to the St Ives life-boat crew for the rescue of the crew of the *Alba*. Five members of that year-old rescue lost their lives that day.

Such a disaster in a small station strikes hard. There was scarcely a person in St Ives who was not involved. Wives were left without husbands, sisters without brothers, and mothers without sons. Each of the seven men who lost their lives was married, and eight children were left fatherless. One of the wives was expecting a child. On that stormy winter's night the coxswain's wife had lost her husband and her son.

Coxswain Cocking was an experienced and fearless life-boatman. He had been a member of the St Ives life-boat crew for many years, and had been coxswain for the past ten. He was a fine leader of men. People in St Ives said that nothing would have stopped him from taking the life-boat out that night, and such were his powers of leadership that the crew followed him willingly and unquestioningly.

The Institution awarded William Freeman the bronze medal, and posthumously awarded bronze medals to the other seven members of the crew. The wives and dependants of those who were lost were all paid a pension by the Institution as if their men had been killed on active service.

This is the price which is sometimes—though mercifully very seldom—paid by those who man the life-boats, and it is a price which each and every life-boatman is fully aware of every time he answers a call of distress.

The crew duck for cover as the Cromer life-boat hits the water at the foot of the slipway

Coxswain Tom King of St Helier, Jersey, the first post-war winner of the Institution's gold medal. See chapter XI

Coxswain Richard Evans, the winner of the only other gold medal awarded since the end of the war. See chapter XI

CHAPTER SEVEN

Life-boats at War

War for the second time in a quarter of a century broke out between Britain and Germany on 3 September 1939, and the R.N.L.I. almost immediately began to feel the strain on its resources. Not only were calls on the life-boats more frequent and in many cases more arduous than ever before, but younger members of crews were called up for active service, and many of the life-boats had to be manned throughout the war by men who were recalled from retirement.

Added to this were the dangers of enemy action at sea, the black-out when all the distinguishing features of the coastline disappeared at night and no guiding lights were shown, and defence regulations which made entry and exit to harbours difficult and sometimes impossible. Not only were the crews shorn of their younger men, but many of the men in control at headquarters were active officers in the Naval Services and the Institution was deprived of their invaluable advice and help. Materials for repairing life-boats became more and more difficult to obtain as the needs of the fighting services took over.

The first seven months of the war were known as the 'phoney' war, for on land at least it hardly seemed as if there was a war on. Everything seemed suspended in a breathless hush and many people began to think that perhaps there might not be a war at all.

On the sea things were very different. Our coastline had been suddenly ringed with mines, already the German navy was beginning to attack our shipping, Coastal Command flew constantly over the seas to keep watch for enemy action, and the calls on the life-boat service were frequent. Crashed aircraft gave the life-boatmen many hours of fruitless searching throughout the war. Air-sea rescue services went to the assistance of aircraft coming down far out at sea, but nearer the shore it was often the life-boat which performed the search.

On one occasion the Margate life-boat saved a pilot who had come down in the sea. He was thoroughly exhausted and badly burnt when they found him, for he had been in the sea for over an hour while the life-boat searched in mist. They brought him safely back to Margate. His name was Richard Hillary and he was the four-times great nephew of Sir William Hillary, founder of the Shipwreck Institution.

The life-boat service had never been so busy, and to add to the dangers the winter of 1939–40 was one of the hardest on record. Reports from coxswains spoke of seaspray freezing as it fell and of life-boat crews having to chip ice off their oilskins before they could take them off after coming back from service.

One of the worst difficulties was that of darkness. Before the war when a life-boat was called out at night, acetylene flares lit the scene in a bright glow at the boathouse and on the slipway, enabling launchers to see what they were doing and allowing the coxswain to see when his boat reached the water when running down the slipway from the boathouse. Now all this had to be done in the darkness. An occasional quick flash from a hand torch was a poor substitute for the light they had known before.

Maroons were silenced. The crew of the life-boat had to be summoned individually when a call came through. To begin with even wireless silence was imposed, for by now many life-boats were equipped with radio. Life-boat crews might listen but they were not allowed to speak. This lasted for the first four months of the war and then the rigid ruling was relaxed, but life-boats still had to be extremely careful what they said in case information of any kind was given to the enemy.

Navigation in those days was difficult. Not only was it impossible in the darkness to pinpoint a life-boat's position by the guiding lights of beacons, lighthouses and lights on the shore, but minefields were laid all round the coast, especially at the entrances to big ports, and the positions of these had to be known and the channels through them remembered. A coxswain's responsibilities, already very great, were more than doubled.

Furthermore, discipline was suddenly imposed. One of the main reasons for the Institution remaining independent of government support was that it was free to manage its own affairs, but now the entire coastline was controlled by the Royal Navy and no boat—including the life-boat—could be launched without the permission of the naval officer in charge. This was natural in the system of defence, but gradually the Institution found itself being involved in further mounds of orders, demands and restrictions. Naval officers began ordering life-boats out. Unfamiliar with the well-tried system of life-saving practised by the Institution they issued orders to coxswains which were incorrect, sometimes dangerous, and often too late to be of any use. Eventually it was agreed that although the Navy might give or withhold permission for launching a life-boat, the actual order to launch must remain the right of the Institution alone.

All this imposed a considerable strain on the coxswains. They were accustomed to being in absolute control of their boats and they disliked taking orders from others as to what they should or should not do, but they reluctantly realized that in the circumstances there had to be some measure of control.

On some occasions permission for the life-boat to launch was withheld until it was either too late to help, or the rescue was made twice as dangerous as it need have been. This prompted the coxswain of the Buckie life-boat to ask why he should have to wait three hours for permission to go to the help of a crashed aircraft from a man who was lying in his bed in Aberdeen. Many times coxswains turned a blind eye to the regulations and took their life-boats out without obtaining permission. This too had its dangers. No lights were shown on the life-boat, and an unidentified vessel approaching the shore was liable to be fired on by the coastal defence batteries. Sometimes life-boats returned from service under a hail of bullets from our own side.

But on the whole the system worked reasonably well and there was close co-operation between the Navy and the R.N.L.I. The service never lacked fuel, despite the desperate shortage, and considering the fact that the Institution was using 50,000 gallons of fuel a year this was a great help. Also the Admiralty did not call up men without whom it would be impossible for a life-boat station to function, although throughout the war life-boats operated with reduced crews and those very much over age.

The R.N.L.I. took an active part in what was described as 'the miracle of Dunkirk'. In May 1940, with the German army closing in on Dunkirk from all sides, the call came suddenly and urgently for the little boats—the pleasure steamers, the motor cruisers and the holiday yachts—to go to the rescue of the British Expeditionary Force and the French Army, fighting desperately to maintain a tiny foothold on French soil and keep the last remaining port available to them open. Every vessel that could float was needed. When the call came from the Admiralty the life-boats were summoned too, and from Shoreham Harbour in Sussex to Great Yarmouth and Gorleston in Norfolk the life-boats assembled at Dover and sailed to help in the evacuation of the men from France. They came from Ramsgate, Margate, Great Yarmouth and Gorleston, Lowestoft, Southwold, Aldeburgh, Walton and Frinton, Clacton, Southend-on-Sea, Walmer, Hythe, Dungeness, Hastings, Eastbourne, Newhaven, Shoreham Harbour and Poole and Bournemouth. There was also a new life-boat which had just been completed and had not yet been named. Apart from the Ramsgate and Margate boats which left early with their own crews, they were taken over by the Navy and manned by Naval officers and men. This caused a considerable amount of ill-feeling amongst the life-boatmen, most of whom had been prepared to go themselves, but this was an emergency and there was no time to argue the case. ·

Most of the work of the life-boats was taking men off the beaches and ferrying them to the bigger ships lying out in deeper water. With the land battle raging closer and closer, and with German aircraft constantly harrying them with bombs and machine gun fire it is impossible to estimate how many men the life-boats took off, but even after Dunkirk was finally abandoned to the Germans and the 300,000 men were safely home, the life-boats' work was not finished. Many of the men had put to sea from Dunkirk in anything that would float rather than be taken prisoner, and the life-boats spent a long time searching for them and rescuing them. The coxswains of the

Ramsgate and Margate life-boats were both awarded the Distinguished Service Medal for their part in this rescue. Of the life-boats taking part in the epic of Dunkirk only one failed to return home.

CHAPTER EIGHT

Arranmore—1940

The line gun and the breeches buoy form the most important aid to life-saving known, and particularly during the war these two devices between them saved many hundreds of lives. It is worth while tracing their origin and development.

As long ago as 1796 experiments were taking place in the hope of finding some means of firing a line from the shore to a wreck, and these experiments seem to have been started simultaneously by an English soldier, Sergeant Bell, and by a Frenchman called La Fère. Little is known about the form their respective experiments took, but there can be no doubt that these were the first attempts to develop the rocket apparatus.

The first practical experiments, however, were carried out by a Captain George William Manby who was born near Dereham Market in Norfolk in 1765. He joined the Army and eventually became Barrack Master at Yarmouth. For some time he had experimented casually with the idea of a line fired from one point to another point some distance away, but it was in February 1807 that he was prompted to take up his researches in earnest. At that time a vessel was wrecked on Yarmouth beach. She was the gun-brig *Snipe*, and of her crew sixty were drowned. This disaster set Manby on the road to the invention of the mortar apparatus. He realized that had there been some effective means of conveying a line to the *Snipe* most of those who lost their lives might have been saved, for the wreck took place only sixty yards from the shore.

Manby established the first mortar station at Yarmouth and proved the success of his apparatus by saving seven lives from a wreck the following year. By 1824 there were forty-five of these stations round the coast and they had saved over two hundred lives. This was the year in which the Shipwreck Institution was founded, and steps were taken by the Institution to supply mortar apparatus to various stations round the coast. However, by 1854, when the Institution first received a government subsidy because of its financial difficulties, the control of shore life-saving stations was taken out of the Institution's hands, and to this day remains in the control of the government.

Gradually improvements were made on the mortar apparatus. Then a Helston man, Henry Trengrouse, made the first experiments with a rocket to fire a line in 1821. This principle was far simpler and more effective than the clumsy mortar system, and although Trengrouse's rocket had a number of faults and was never used, it set others on the way to perfecting the rocket apparatus. A rocket could fire a line further, especially after the introduction of the double rocket. This allowed the first rocket to carry the line upwards and outwards and then the first rocket fired the second, which carried the line still further on its way. Gradually the line-gun carried on life-boats today was evolved.

Although much work had gone into methods of firing a line from the shore to a wreck there still remained the problem of what to do once the line got there. Manby invented a life-cot—a kind of canvas raft—which could be pulled between the wreck and the shore, but this was not successful, and in fact it was not until the invention of the supremely simple breeches buoy that the actual business of taking men off a wreck was satisfactorily solved.

The breeches buoy was invented by a Lieutenant Kisbee, and consists of a life-belt with a framework underneath into which a man can thrust his legs as he would do into a pair of breeches. When the line is fired from a life-boat to a wreck, a block is attached to the end of the line on the life-boat. Through this block runs an endless rope. The men on the wreck pull on the line fired to them and draw the block across. The block has a tail which is attached to any convenient part of the wreck at a reasonable height from the water. The breeches buoy is attached to the endless rope on the life-boat, and by pulling the rope through the block the breeches buoy is hauled over to the wreck.

Once those on the wreck receive the breeches buoy one man at a time—or in an emergency, two—climbs into it. Then the life-boatmen pull the breeches buoy with the man in it across. Being on part of an endless line the breeches buoy can shuttle backwards and forwards between the life-boat and the wreck as often as is necessary.

After the evacuation of Dunkirk the Germans began to try to starve us into submission. Submarines ringed our coast, and one by one the sea lanes became too dangerous to use. The convoy system, whereby merchant ships sailed in large groups under the watchful eye of warships, was operated. On the safe arrival and departure of these convoys our life blood depended. Food and war material flowed into Britain from America and Canada, but in ever decreasing amounts. The inadequately protected merchant ships had to run the submarine blockade and at one stage during the height of the Battle of the Atlantic the only passage left open for convoys was between Northern Ireland and Scotland.

Now the Irish Free State was neutral, but the Institution's law that all men of all nationalities should be the objects of the life-boats' work held true throughout the war.

December 1940, and the convoys which supplied Britain were battling through. They had to contend not only with the menace of the German U-boats but with the weather as well. The gale had been rising for three days and was now blowing at hurricane force from the north-west. The wind brought blinding snow with it. A convoy from America was heading for the passage, and picked up the light on Tory Island off the extreme north-west of the neutral Irish mainland. Shortly afterwards a Dutch steamer, the *Stolwijk*, lost her rudder in the heavy seas and began to drift southwards with the wind towards a string of islands. She was helpless in the wind and sea and soon struck a reef of rock between two of the islands. A destroyer from the convoy tried to rescue her crew but failed, and lost four of her own men in the attempt. Ten of the Dutch crew managed to launch a boat from the *Stolwijk*, but it capsized and all ten were drowned.

The *Stolwijk* was in amongst a string of small islands in the darkness, the nearest life-boat station was twenty-five miles away, and the vessel was being pounded to death by the seas.

At dawn the Arranmore life-boat put out. Coxswain John Boyle did not know exactly where the *Stolwijk* lay, but he knew she must be near Tory Island, so he made for that position. The Atlantic waves, unhindered in their progress across hundreds of miles of open sea, rode down majestically on the life-boat, tossing her around like a rubber ball, and it was not until mid-day that she rounded Bloody Foreland and saw the *Stolwijk*. Her bows were under water, the seas were breaking over her, and at her stern the life-boatmen could see the tiny dots of men waiting for the inevitable end. The tide was running out between the islands on which the *Stolwijk* was wrecked against the force of the gale, and the sea was terribly confused all round the vessel.

The coxswain took the life-boat between two of the islands and got to leeward. He dared not approach too closely to the *Stolwijk* because of the sea. He put out his anchor and then allowed the tide to carry the life-boat down towards the wreck, paying out the anchor cable as he did so. He approached as near as he dared and then made the cable fast. By now he was near enough to fire a gun line even against the force of the gale. The Dutch crew on board the *Stolwijk* caught the line as it came over, pulled the block aboard and made it fast, despite the fact that they must have been numbed with cold, having been on the deck for over twelve hours in that weather.

One by one they climbed into the breeches buoy and the life-boatmen pulled them over. It took at least five minutes to haul each man in. The distance varied between 40 and 80 yards. Twice the line carrying the breeches buoy snapped from being rubbed against a broken plate on the *Stolwijk*'s side, and each time a man was in the breeches buoy. He was hauled in through the water, and then the coxswain had to manœuvre the life-boat into position for the gun to be fired again. The third time the gun firer discovered that the cartridge box had been left open. There were four cartridges left and they had been soaked by the sea. There were still three men left on the wreck.

Anxiously the gun firer loaded the gun and fired. The cartridge did not explode. Neither did the second. Nor did the third. The lives of the three men on the *Stolwijk* depended on the last cartridge. There was little hope for them. Every man on the life-boat watched tensely as the last cartridge was loaded, and they saw the gun firer take careful aim and watched his hand tighten on the trigger. Even if the cartridge fired, the line must carry true to the *Stolwijk*.

There was a sharp report and a puff of smoke blown instantly away by the gale. The last cartridge had fired and the men in the life-boat watched the iron rod with the line attached to it travelling straight and true, the line snaking easily out of its container on the deck, to land across the stern of the *Stolwijk*. The last three men were taken off.

By now it was five o'clock in the afternoon, and it was midnight before the life-boat regained her station. The rescue of eighteen men had taken over sixteen hours, and when the lifeboat reached the shelter of her station on Aran Island the rescued men and the life-boat's crew themselves had to be helped out of the boat. During the four hours of the actual rescue the crew had worked without their oilskins on, for they had hampered movement too much.

Coxswain John Boyle was awarded not only the Institution's gold medal for gallantry for this rescue, but also a gold medal by Queen Wilhelmina of the Netherlands. It was one of the many outstanding rescues of the second world war.

CHAPTER NINE

Cromer—1941

Of the Institution's active fleet of over 150 life-boats very nearly half are launched down slipways, and this is undoubtedly the easiest and quickest method of launching. But it is only possible to provide a life-boat with a slipway where the conditions are right. The boathouse has to stand high out of the water, either on a ledge of rock or on the end of a pier, and where the shore is flat or there are no suitable heights on which to build a boathouse this is not possible. The slipway itself must be protected from the weather and there must be at least six feet of reasonably sheltered water at the foot of it to receive the life-boat safely at the lowest possible tide.

The slipway has a gradient as steep as 1 in 4, and the life-boat sliding down it may hit the water at a speed of anything up to thirty miles an hour.

The life-boat sits in the boathouse with its bows facing the double doors which, when opened, lead on to the slipway. The boat is secured by a slip chain forward, and by a wire attached to a shoe at the stern of the boat. This wire runs to the winch engine at the very back of the boathouse. When the call to launch the life-boat comes the chain is loosened and the weight of the boat is taken by the winch wire. The winch engine is operated by a shore helper who allows the boat to slide out of the boathouse on to the slipway where the mast is set up and the radio aerial erected. The position down the slipway from which the life-boat is launched depends on the state of the weather and the tide.

Then when the order to launch is given to the helpers in the boathouse by the coxswain the winch wire is knocked out of the shoe and the boat travels down the slipway into the water.

When she returns after a service the life-boat is pulled up the slipway stern first by the winching engine until she regains the boathouse where she is properly secured. This is a tricky operation and may take some time, but there is no need for hurry on a return from service. Sometimes the weather is too bad for the life-boat to be rehoused on her return, in which case she will usually make for some sheltered port until conditions will allow her to go back to her station.

The only drawback to launching down a slipway is the cost of building the boathouse and the slipway itself, which is considerably higher than keeping a boat moored in a harbour or even launching her with a tractor. Nevertheless it is by far the quickest method of launching, and during the war it became increasingly necessary to launch quickly.

Cromer lies on the Norfolk coast, a popular seaside resort in the summer months. But some miles out to sea lies a series of treacherous sandbanks where the depth of the water sometimes varies by as much as sixty feet in a few yards. These sandbanks have been the ruin of many fine ships.

Cromer has two life-boat stations. The Number Two life-boat is housed behind the beach and is towed to the sea by a tractor. The Number One life-boat, the bigger one, is housed at the very end of Cromer pier, beyond the promenade where fishermen wait peacefully for their catches and the pavilion where holidaymakers are entertained.

There is a map in the boathouse showing the position of the various sandbanks and big-headed pins mark the positions of wrecks. The map is peppered with pins. Here the 46-foot Watson-type life-boat is housed, its wheel set unusually amidships. The Cromer life-boat was one of the first to have her wheel placed there, and it was found to be so suitable that now more life-boats are being constructed in the same way. The name of this life-boat is *Henry Blogg*.

And there in itself is a story.

The life-boat is called after the late coxswain-superintendent of the Cromer life-boat station. This is a unique title, because it meant that the coxswain was in charge of both life-boats and could choose whichever one he wished if the life-boat was called to the rescue. The life-boat's name is a living monument to the man who was the greatest coxswain of all time—the greatest of the great.

It is impossible to deal shortly with the life of Henry Blogg. A list of his awards will give some idea of the kind of man he was. He won the Institution's gold medal for great gallantry three times, a feat only equalled by Sir William Hillary, the Institution's founder. He won the silver medal four times. He won the George Cross and the British Empire Medal. And he won the Canine Defence League's silver medal for the rescue of a dog from a wreck. He served with the Cromer life-boat for fifty-three years, the last thirty-eight of them as coxswain. He was called out on service 387 times and rescued 873 lives.

This is the record of the man who was described as 'Cromer's greatest son', and at whose funeral in 1954 thousands waited in the rain outside the church to pay their last respects as the cortège passed by.

It is difficult to single out any one of Henry Blogg's epic rescues. If you choose one you miss out a dozen equally inspiring, for he was a man who inspired confidence and trust. Who else could encourage a crew with an average age of over fifty during the first world war to man a pulling life-boat for fourteen hours with hardly a break? He was a quiet man who hated publicity of any kind, a man of few words, but those were words which spoke volumes, and yet he had that indefinable quality of leadership which all those who worked under him recognized, admired and obeyed.

One of the rescues which was typical of the courage and endurance of this man happened during the war, and yet for this rescue he was only awarded the silver medal. I spoke to several of the men who served under Henry Blogg on this service and I expressed surprise that he did not receive the gold medal.

One of them smiled.

'Ah, but you see Henry had got his third gold medal only a few months before,' he said. 'If they'd given him another one it might have looked like favouritism!'

The s.s. *English Trader* went aground on one of the sandbanks about twenty-two miles from Cromer called Hammond Knoll on 26 October 1941. At this time during the war, as we have seen, the R.N.L.I. was controlled to some extent by the Royal Navy, and it was the naval station at Great Yarmouth which asked the life-boat to go out to the *English Trader* which had a crew of forty-nine. A gale was blowing from the north-east, there were squalls of rain, sleet and hail, it was bitterly cold and the seas were mountainous. Frightening conditions, but conditions which the crews of the life-boats are well used to.

At this time Henry Blogg was sixty-five years old, which is normally retiring age for a life-boat coxswain, but due to the shortage of men during the war and also to his own excellent health and unsurpassed record Henry Blogg worked on.

The life-boat *H. F. Bailey* left the slipway soon after eight o'clock that Sunday morning with a crew of twelve. Some idea of the fact that life-boat work is often a family affair can be gained from the fact that eight members of the crew had the surname Davies.

It took the life-boat nearly three and a half hours to reach Hammond Knoll, and there they found the *English Trader*. Coxswain Blogg declared afterwards that he had never been faced with such a difficult problem. Her hull was almost under water and the sea was sweeping over her from both bow and stern, meeting in a tremendous crash of water over the vessel and pouring down on top of her. So heavy were the seas that at times only the vessel's masts were visible. Her derricks had broken loose and were swinging wildly with the movement of the ship, making an approach alongside a very dangerous proposition. Her hatches had been torn off, her cargo was being thrown out of her holds as though gigantic invisible hands were flinging things in all directions. All round the ship crates and bales and pieces of wreckage littered the water. And in the middle of this chaos forty-four men were huddled in the stricken vessel's chartroom which offered the best shelter there was. The five other members of the crew had already been swept overboard and drowned.

Coxswain Blogg tried to run alongside the vessel, but the sea breaking over her made it impossible to get near enough. A line was fired to try to reach the ship, but the wind blew it straight back again.

Henry Blogg knew the conditions here as no other man did,

and for the time being he allowed the sea to have its way. He ordered Signalman Walter Allen to signal to the captain of the *English Trader* that he would make another attempt to come alongside at slack water, which would be about four o'clock, and the life-boat stood off from the crippled vessel to wait. This did not mean that the life-boat crew had nothing to do. It was a continuous exhausting fight to keep the life-boat's head to the sea to prevent her from being swamped or capsized. Coxswain Blogg was not admitting defeat: he was merely biding his time, but to some of the younger, more impetuous members of the crew he appeared to be wasting it, and as they saw the terrible pounding the *English Trader* was receiving they urged him to try again.

For the only time in his life Henry Blogg agreed to someone else's request against his own better judgment. And it was soon to be proved that he was right and the others wrong.

Coxswain Blogg tried to manœuvre the life-boat towards the *English Trader* again. The conditions were such that he was forced to make his approach broadside on. When they were within a quarter of a mile of the vessel a huge sea bore down on them. Coxswain Blogg described it as a 'huge wall of water'. Someone shouted a warning and at that moment the sea swallowed them.

The life-boat heeled over on to her beam ends. The men on the *English Trader* saw her keel come right out of the water; and the *H. F. Bailey* was not a self-righter. Five of the crew, some of whom had been working their way forward to put out fenders for the life-boat's approach to the *English Trader*, were swept overboard. Two others managed to cling on. Coxswain Blogg was lifted up as though he had been a cork and flung into the sea. The second coxswain went too. By a miracle the life-boat righted herself and those left in the boat hurried to the help of those in the water. Jack Davies, the son of the second coxswain, took the wheel. One by one the men were brought back aboard the life-boat. They were all wearing life-jackets and to pull men so encumbered and heavy with water over the projecting gunwale of the life-boat taxed the strength and endurance of those men left aboard. It took five minutes to haul each man in. First came Second Coxswain J. J. Davies, and then Coxswain

Blogg. Barely giving himself time to regain his breath the sixty-five-year-old coxswain took the wheel again, and the three other men were brought aboard. The last man, Signalman Walter Allen, had been in the water for twenty-five minutes. When the life-boat reached him he was unconscious and the rest of the crew were so exhausted that the two mechanics had to leave their engines in order to pull him aboard.

The men took him to the cabin and began artificial respiration. They removed his mittens to chafe his hands to restore the circulation. For a time nothing happened, then at last Walter Allen revived. He sat up and asked for his mittens as though he intended to get back to work, but almost immediately he collapsed and died.

When Coxswain Blogg was told of Signalman Allen's death he refused to believe it at first, and then came a feeling of deep shock, for this was the first time he had ever lost a man. Walter Allen had served aboard the life-boat for nearly forty years. His death was a bitter blow to the entire crew.

The coxswain took stock of the situation. They had now been out for nearly seven hours and the crew were exhausted. The engines had stalled when the life-boat heeled to the sea, and when Motor Mechanic H. W. Davies restarted them and tried to engage the gears they stalled again. It was clear what had happened. Loose ropes swept from the life-boat's deck had fouled the propellers. Desperately he restarted the engines and engaged gear but the engines stalled again.

Motor Mechanic Davies worked furiously at the engines while the life-boat drifted. Starting and stopping each engine in turn, ramming them viciously into gear, he managed to give the life-boat some way. He succeeded, but it took a quarter of an hour of hard work on each engine.

But although the engines at last responded the ropes were still there. Speed was reduced and it was almost impossible to steer. Coxswain Blogg decided to return to Great Yarmouth, as the weather was too bad to rehouse the boat at Cromer. They could do nothing more for the *English Trader* at that time.

They radioed for a doctor and an ambulance to meet them and set a course for Great Yarmouth. Meanwhile the Great Yarmouth and Gorleston life-boat had been launched and was

The St Ives life-boat being drawn back on to its launching carriage after
returning from service

The new life-boathouse at Selsey. The catwalk to the old boathouse can be seen
in the background. The life-boat itself stands on the slipway

MAST HEAD SIGNALLING LIGHT

AERIAL

DROGUE FAIRLEAD

PROPELLER SCUTTLE

CLEAR VIEW SCREEN

STARB'D LIGHT & SCREEN

MAST CRUTCH

DOUBLE-BOTTOM AIR VENTS

LIFEBUOY

RADIO CONTROL

COMPASS

2ND MECHANICS SEAT

CHIEF MECHANIC'S SEAT

AIR INTAKE

PORT ENGINE REVERSE WHEEL

REDUCING GEAR

STEAMING LIGHT

FLOODLIGHT

EXHAUST OUTLET

AERIAL LEAD IN

WATERTIGHT DOOR

HATCH TO FUEL COMPT.

SCUPPER

ENGINE-DRIVEN CAPSTAN HEAD

CABIN HATCH

ENGINES: TWO 4LW GARDNER DIESEL UNITS

FUEL TANK

ENGINE ROOM INNER BOTTOM

LONGITUDINAL WING BULKHEADS

PROPELLERS SET IN TUNNELS

LOUD HAILER

AIR CASES

ANCHOR STOWED

PROVISION LKR.

CHART CONTAINER

BATTERY BOX

CABIN SEAT

TRANSVERSE BULKHEADS

R.N.L.B. WILLIAM TAYLOR OF OLDHAM

RECEIVER & TRANSMITTER

RH LH

This diagram vividly shows the superb design of the modern 46-foot Watson-type life-boat making for the *English Trader*. The life-boat tried to get along-side the vessel, and on one occasion managed to get a line aboard her, but this soon parted. The captain of the *English Trader* signalled the life-boat to leave them, and as the seas were increasing and darkness was falling they did. It was war time and they could show no lights to aid them in the rescue, and they returned to Great Yarmouth.

At six o'clock in the evening the Cromer life-boat reached Great Yarmouth. The crew were so exhausted that they had to be helped ashore. They were taken to the Shipwrecked Sailors' Home and given hot baths, food and dry clothes. But Coxswain Blogg had no time for rest. He rang through to Cromer and asked for more clothing to be sent over and another signalman to come and replace Walter Allen. Signalman George Cox immediately volunteered to take Walter Allen's place and came with the clothing by car straight away.

Coxswain Blogg supervised the refuelling of the life-boat. Motor Mechanic Davies also had little time for rest. As soon as the life-boat arrived he began the arduous job of clearing the ropes from the propellers, for all the crew knew that although Henry Blogg had brought them back to Great Yarmouth they had not finished their attempt to rescue the forty-four men on the *English Trader*. When Coxswain Blogg had set his mind on something nothing would move him from it.

And in this case it was just as well.

During the war a boom—a kind of barrier—was raised across the entrance to Great Yarmouth harbour for defence purposes. If a vessel wished to enter or leave the harbour the boom had to be lowered to the sea bed, and after the vessel had passed it was raised again. The Admiral in charge had left orders that in view of the weather no vessel was to go out and that the boom was not to be lowered.

This was Coxswain Blogg's next job. He got in touch with the duty officer and somehow, with that quality of command that was always in his presence, he persuaded the duty officer to ignore the Admiral's orders and lower the boom to allow the life-boat to leave.

At a quarter past four in the morning, with some ropes still fouling the propellers, the *H. F. Bailey* slipped out of Great

Yarmouth harbour and headed again for the *English Trader*. The weather was the same as it had been the previous day although the wind and sea had gone down very slightly. It was a dangerous and arduous journey. There were no beacons lit to give warning of the many sandbanks in their path, and Coxswain Blogg had to steer by instinct and his own sure knowledge of local conditions. The life-boat had twenty-two miles and three hours of darkness to battle against the full fury of the gale.

At eight o'clock in the morning the life-boat reached the *English Trader*. Her fore part was under water now, but the sea had gone down a little, and Coxswain Blogg brought the life-boat alongside. Within half an hour the crew of forty-four were taken off.

The weather was still too bad to rehouse the life-boat at Cromer, so they took the survivors to Great Yarmouth and landed them there.

So ended one of Henry Blogg's greatest rescues. For a man of sixty-five to undertake such a service was remarkable enough. But to have the qualities to undergo being thrown into a raging sea and then take command of the life-boat again; to urge his exhausted crew to further efforts and go out again from Great Yarmouth; to persuade the naval authorities at Great Yarmouth to ignore the orders of the Admiral in charge; to work for about twenty-seven hours with little or no rest, serve to show the extraordinary qualities of the man who can truly be described as the greatest coxswain of all time.

CHAPTER TEN

Newcastle—1942

Wartime imposed great strains on the Institution. A fleet which had been adequate in 1939 could scarcely be expected to withstand the demands made on it during the next six years. In the first year of the war alone life-boats were called out on service 1,000 times, yet there was no chance of adding to the fleet or improving it. Coxswains simply had to make do with the boats they had when war broke out, and with crews, boats and equipment inadequate for the demands made on them they performed magnificent work. It is the story of one such life-boat that we come to now.

By 1942 the submarine menace was just as great as it had been, although by now it was being controlled. Nevertheless the convoy system was still in operation and the dangers to shipping were still very great.

It was January 1942, and a convoy from Liverpool was heading for the same passage between Scotland and Ireland that the convoys had used for so long. There was a south-easterly gale blowing behind it and somehow in the darkness of that winter's night one of the ships in the convoy had gone off course. She struck five miles away from the Cloughey life-boat station in County Down. The life-boat was launched immediately and found the vessel stuck high on the rocks and in no danger, but as the life-boat turned the coxswain saw several more vessels following the course of the wrecked ship. He immediately set a course for them to warn them of their danger, but he was too late. They struck. The coxswain saw a destroyer heading in the same direction and he flashed his lamp at her in warning. The destroyer sent up star-shells when she saw his signal. By their light she saw the life-boat and headed safely out to sea again.

The life-boat waited, but no more ships followed those already on the rocks; but stretched out along a mile and a half of the shore seven ships were now lying stranded. In those dark convoy days with no lights showing, each vessel followed the one in front, and if one ship veered off course it was more than possible that several more would do so too before the mistake was discovered.

All seven ships were so far on the rocks that the life-boat was powerless to help. Only one was not lying high and dry, and the life-boat stood by while her crew tried to refloat her.

Meanwhile the coastguard had asked the Newcastle station, twenty miles to the south, to stand by, and the crew had done so until three o'clock in the morning. Then a further message came from the coastguard to say that four ships had struck, not just one as had been previously thought. The Newcastle life-boat was launched immediately this news came through. The boat was one of the oldest in the Institution's fleet, a light, open boat weighing under six tons. In calm seas she could carry her crew of seven and forty-five men, and in rough weather no more than twenty-eight. These statistics are important in view of what was about to take place.

The life-boat had twenty miles to travel with the gale behind her. The sea was very rough and there were squally showers of sleet and rain, and the wind was rising still further.

At five o'clock in the morning she reached the scene and headed straight for a Liverpool steamer, the *Browning*, which lay furthest out. Coxswain Patrick Murphy did not see the Cloughey life-boat at all. Earlier the *Browning* had refused assistance from the Cloughey boat, but now the tide was flowing and heavy seas were breaking over her. Already a shore life-saving team had managed to take off seventeen men, but the incoming tide had pushed the rescuers too far back for them to take off any more.

The coxswain anchored his life-boat to windward and dropped down to her on his cable, but the seas were so rough that although he tried for an hour to approach the *Browning* he was beaten back every time. He asked the captain of the *Browning* if there was enough water to leeward for the life-boat, and the captain told him that there was.

Now the *Browning*'s stern was fast on a reef and her bows were very close to the rocks on the shore. Coxswain Murphy would have to take the life-boat between the bows of the steamer and the rocks. The channel between the two varied in width from sixteen to twenty feet, and the life-boat was nine feet wide. There was very little margin for error in those conditions for the life-boat to get through unscathed. At the right moment Coxswain Murphy called for full speed, and the life-boat charged through the channel unhurt, although at one point a man could have leant out at one side and touched the bows of the steamer while another man leant out the other side and touched the rocks.

Now the water was quiet, with the steamer's side cutting off the wind, but the pool in which the life-boat found herself was very small. Twenty-nine men clambered down from the steamer's deck into the life-boat—one more than her maximum for safety in the weather—and there were still ten men left on board. These extra men would load the life-boat so heavily that her gunwale would be only two feet above the water line. Coxswain Murphy calculated the risk. If he did not take the men off they would undoubtedly die. If he did the chances were very strong that they would all die in any case. He called on them to come aboard and they did so.

The life-boat was very small and, weighed down by the number of men in her, she was riding low in the water. Men were crammed into every available space, some sitting on each other, some standing, and the worst part of the journey was still to come.

There was no room in that pool of calm water to turn the life-boat to get out through the channel they had entered by. The only chance was to go out astern of the *Browning*, over the reef of rocks on which the stern lay. Coxswain Murphy looked at the crowded life-boat. He looked at the water lapping two feet below the gunwale and he looked at the water breaking white over the reef. He had no idea how deep that water was.

He watched and waited. A big sea advanced towards the reef, and as it began to rise over the rocks he called to the mechanic for full speed. The life-boat shot forward over the reef and into the whirling madness of the storm-swept water once more, borne over the reef by the wave and two more which followed it.

They could not return to Newcastle in that gale with the

life-boat so overloaded, so Coxswain Murphy headed for the fishing village of Portavogie, and here he landed his survivors. Six of them were taken to hospital, and the rest were cared for by the villagers themselves. Even with his lightened boat Coxswain Murphy would not take her back to Newcastle in that gale, and he and the crew returned by land. They reached home seventeen hours after they had left.

Coxswain Murphy was awarded the gold medal for this service, another of the outstanding war services by an Irish life-boat.

CHAPTER ELEVEN

St Helier—1949

There are two life-boat stations in the Channel Islands, one at St Peter Port on Guernsey and the other at St Helier on Jersey. After the collapse of France the Institution ordered that these two life-boats should sail for Cowes on the Isle of Wight if a German invasion took place. On 29 June 1940 invasion was imminent and the order came. The station at St Helier had not got a crew to man the life-boat, so the Institution asked the St Peter Port life-boat to go for her. The St Peter Port boat was a reserve boat, for the life-boat itself happened to be at Cowes for an overhaul at this time.

The boat reached St Helier as the German attack on the Channel Islands was beginning. The life-boat was machine-gunned and the coxswain's son, who was a member of the crew, was killed.

The Governor of Jersey announced that he wanted to keep the St Helier life-boat. Doubtless he foresaw times in the future when the life-boat would be badly needed, and true to the principles of the Institution that life-boats should be available for all men at all times, headquarters in London agreed.

The St Peter Port life-boat returned to Guernsey and remained there throughout the war, though she was not used for life-saving purposes. At the end of the war she was found to be in such bad shape that she could no longer be used and she was scrapped.

Meanwhile the St Peter Port life-boat itself was sent from Cowes to an auxiliary station at Killybegs in County Donegal in Ireland. Many of these auxiliary stations were opened by the Institution on the Irish coast during the war to counteract the great pressure put on the life-boat service there, and the St Peter Port life-boat served at Killybegs for the duration.

After this little was heard of the two life-boat stations in the

Channel Islands, and the Institution had no idea at that time what had happened to its life-boats, but three years later the honorary secretary of the St Helier station managed to get a message through to the Institution which successfully told the officials something of what had happened. It was written on a printed German Red Cross form and read:

"Greetings to all. Often go out with Howard, Dee and the boys. Howard sends regards to Groves and Guttridge and hopes to see them soon."

To the German authorities this must have seemed an innocent if slightly unnecessary message, but to the Institution it meant a great deal. The St Helier life-boat's name was *Howard D* and she had been built by a firm called Groves and Guttridge on the Isle of Wight. So this seemingly innocent message in fact told the Institution that the life-boat was still working and all was well with her crew.

After the war it was discovered that the crew of the St Helier life-boat had been employed throughout the war on a full-time basis, and that they had been out on service at least five times. 27 people had been rescued, eight of them from the s.s. *Diamond*, which had been carrying German troops from Granville on the north coast of France to St Helier.

It seems that, true to the Institution's law, the life-boat had been used impartially for the rescue of British and Germans alike.

They must have been difficult days for the crew of the St Helier life-boat, trying to operate a service for humanity which the Nazi regime could not fully understand, but it was four years after the end of the war that the St Helier life-boat performed a service of quite exceptional courage.

The telephone shrilled loudly and urgently in the life-boat station at St Helier. The assistant honorary secretary, Mr K. L. E. Budden, answered it. It was Jersey airport to say that a French military aircraft was reported as having come down in the sea about twenty miles to the south-east. Already ships and aircraft had been alerted: would the life-boat assist in the search?

It was a rough, grey afternoon on 13 September 1949, with a

strong westerly wind blowing. Coxswain Tom King commanded the life-boat. He was at this time sixty-four years old
and was due to retire the following year, a short, stocky man
with a twinkle in his blue eyes and a face rugged with a life
spent facing the sea and storm. He worked as a boatman in
St Helier harbour, a more peaceful job than that of coxswain of
the St Helier life-boat. He had been a seaman all his life and
had sailed with the life-boat since he had manned an oar in the
old pulling and sailing boat. He had been second coxswain all
during the war under the German occupation, and had become
coxswain afterwards in one of the first of the modern life-boats,
the 46-foot *Elizabeth Rippon*. At this particular time the *Elizabeth Rippon* was being refitted, and there was a much older life-
boat with a single screw and auxiliary sail doing temporary
duty at St Helier. She was called *Hearts of Oak*, a name which
was appropriate to what was about to take place.

The crew assembled. They consisted of a fisherman, a civil
servant, a retired boatman of over seventy, a man who ran a
boatyard, a physical training instructor—and, unusually, the
honorary secretary himself, Mr L. P. Stevens. Mr Stevens had
just returned from holiday and had not yet taken over his
duties from his assistant. It is typical of the life-boat service that
although officially he had nothing to do with this particular
service he went as a member of the crew.

The life-boat lies afloat in St Helier harbour. At about
half-past three that afternoon she sailed.

It was a bad day for a search for a missing aircraft. It would
be difficult to imagine a worse one. Rain squalls and fog reduced visibility to a few hundred yards. The life-boat was
buffeted by the tearing winds as she bucked and tossed her way
to the south-east towards the position where the aircraft was
believed to have come down.

Coxswain King took the life-boat to the area, but conditions
were so bad that sometimes visibility was no more than four
hundred yards. They searched for six hours and found nothing.
So often a life-boat is called out on service and finds nothing,
yet the service has to be made and is never refused.

It was learnt later that the aircraft had in fact landed within
the life-boat's area of search and had sunk almost immediately,

taking six members of her crew with her, while three others had managed to get ashore on the French island of Chausey near by.

At half-past nine the life-boat was recalled by a wireless message from St Helier. By then her crew were cold, wet, hungry and very tired, due to the continual buffeting they had received in the heavy seas. Furthermore the life-boat was almost out of fuel. There was clearly nothing more they could do, so the coxswain turned for home.

At midnight they passed the beacon of Demie de Pas which marks the limit of the rocks about two miles from St Helier harbour, and everyone on board was looking forward to getting home for some warmth and dry clothing.

Just after the life-boat passed the beacon another wireless message came through. This message drove all thought of home and warmth from the minds of the crew and led to one of the quickest and bravest rescues ever recorded in the life-boat service.

In a house some miles to the east of St Helier, overlooking the rocky shore, Mr H. J. Norris, the owner, on his way to bed, happened to draw back his curtains to see if there was any sign of an improvement in the weather. There was none, but his eyes were suddenly caught by a light flashing amongst the rocks not very far away where no light should have been. He blinked and rubbed his eyes. The light seemed to be flashing on and off, but this could have been an illusion caused by the rain. And then suddenly he noticed that the flashing was not the sort of intermittent flash which poor visibility might produce. It was flashing slowly and regularly. Three short flashes. Three long flashes. Three short flashes. S.O.S. Again and again the message came through the darkness of the night.

Mr Norris ran to the telephone to ring the police. . . .

The light was also seen by others. Mr R. A. Wagstaffe, living nearby, saw the signals and hastily finding a powerful torch he signalled back to tell the unknown signaller that his message had been received.

And the assistant honorary secretary of the St Helier branch of the R.N.L.I., who happened to be on the pierhead awaiting the return of the life-boat, also saw the light, and hurried to the radio in the life-boat station.

Perhaps because of the weather conditions it was some time before the life-boat could be contacted, but at last the contact was made. An unknown light was flashing a distress signal only a mile or two along the coast. Had the life-boat enough fuel left to go and investigate?

Coxswain King wasn't sure. He had already calculated that there might just be enough fuel to get back into St Helier, but he immediately turned the life-boat and headed for the reported position.

In a short time the life-boat picked up the mysterious light. By now the wind was blowing against the tide and the sea was heavy and treacherous. The rain was falling in gusty squalls. Cautiously the life-boat drew near the light.

The light came from a yacht, the *Maurice Georges*. On board were the owner and two friends with their ten-year-old daughter. They had been to St Malo on the coast of Brittany, and the day before, having heard a reasonable weather forecast for the Channel Islands on the radio, they had decided to return. Nearing St Helier they had run into such bad weather that their speed was drastically reduced, even though they were under sail and engine, and at about eight o'clock in the evening they ran out of fuel. Visibility was so bad that they had no idea where they were, and they decided to drop their anchor and wait until conditions improved. The anchor was dropped, but the weather grew steadily worse until the *Maurice Georges* was pitching and tossing so much that at times she was almost standing upright, and after three hours of this the anchor rope parted. The yacht was now in an extremely dangerous position because when the weather suddenly cleared for a moment they saw to their horror that there were rocks on all sides of them. In desperation the two men on board burnt their shirts to try to attract attention and they sent out S.O.S. messages with their cabin light. It was this light which had been seen on land.

The second anchor was still holding, but only just, and once that parted the yacht would be broken to pieces on the rocks in a matter of minutes. A slender length of rope stood between them and certain death.

They had by now seen the signal from Mr Wagstaffe on the shore telling them that their distress message had been received, but could help reach them in time? It looked unlikely, and the weather was showing no sign of improving. In fact it was getting even worse.

It was in this situation that, unbelievingly, they saw the lights of the life-boat approaching them.

Even the stoutest heart on the life-boat must have missed a beat when they saw what lay before them. All round the distressed vessel the seas were breaking white and angry, there were rocks all round, and although the charts marked these clearly it was so dark that it was almost impossible to pick them out. Yet they were there, some visible, some submerged, ready to tear the bottom out of the life-boat if she should try to get in amongst them. And the life-boat had almost no fuel left. It was quite possible that, having ventured in amongst the rocks, her fuel would run out as the *Maurice Georges*'s had. Furthermore the tide was falling, uncovering more and more rocks as it fell, and the tide around St Helier falls as much as thirty-eight feet. And if any floating wreckage from the *Maurice Georges* should foul their single propeller, they would be as helpless as the yacht itself and suffer the same fate.

But Coxswain King did not hesitate. He ordered two men to take the life-boat's searchlight and go forward with it. They trained it over the bows on to the sea ahead to keep watch for rocks. It was little enough use, but all they could do. Then the coxswain took the life-boat straight in. In the white-capped madness of the sea the life-boat tossed her way in, rocks almost scraping her sides, and indeed at one point the sea seemed their friend. It lifted the life-boat high and then dropped her down again, and, looking aft, the crew could see that it had in fact lifted them clean over a submerged reef.

A line was thrown and caught by the men on the *Maurice Georges*. Normally in these circumstances the life-boat would have edged in close enough to take the crew off the yacht, but this would mean going still further into the seething cauldron around her, and Coxswain King decided to try to tow her out. This would take less time, and with the tide falling time was desperately important.

A tow rope was passed aboard the yacht and made fast, and the life-boat began to edge her way towards the open sea, towing the crippled yacht over and around the terrible rocks.

Sometimes the impossible happens, and it happened in this case. Both the life-boat and the *Maurice Georges* reached the open sea without touching a rock.

The St Helier pilot boat had put out to stand by in case of need, but the life-boat towed the yacht back to St Helier, and when they arrived safely in the harbour the crew of the life-boat saw that the fuel gauge registered nil.

The whole rescue had taken fifteen minutes, a rescue against all probability, a rescue where not only the crew were saved but the yacht itself.

Coxswain Tom King was awarded the gold medal for this rescue, the first gold medal to be awarded since the war.

Some time later the district inspector of the R.N.L.I. came to St Helier to see the place where the *Maurice Georges* had been saved. Coxswain King took the inspector in the life-boat to within a mile of the scene. The inspector asked if they could go in a bit closer as he would like to be able to see the actual situation better. It was a beautiful day with the sea as calm as a mill pond.

Coxswain King's reply was:

'Oh no, sir. I wouldn't like to go in there now. We might hit something.'

CHAPTER TWELVE

Selsey—1956

Since the end of the war there has been an enormous increase in the number of small pleasure craft that take to the water during the summer months. In small ports and harbours all round the coast the white and coloured sails of yachts form a sharp focused splash of colour against the ever-changing blue of the sea. It is a fine form of healthy exercise which is a natural outlet for the instincts which have made the British the greatest nation of seafarers in the world.

But there is a catch in all this. Where the trouble starts is with people who gaily hire a yacht and take it out to sea without the least idea of how to handle it. It is an offence to drive a car on British roads without first obtaining a licence and passing a test, and no one would dream of taking a car on the open roads without first having some lessons from a competent instructor. Yet no such system operates for people going sailing and pleasure cruising. Anyone can hire a boat at any time anywhere, and they are happily left alone to look after it. This naturally causes accidents. Sailing a small yacht, or even rowing a boat, may seem at first glance a great deal easier than driving a car on a busy road, but in fact it is not. Even rowing a boat at sea is very different from rowing one on a lake or pond. Knowledge of winds and tides is essential, and anyone putting out to sea must know how to handle the craft in different conditions and what to do in case of emergencies. Yet year by year the call on the life-boats to go out to the rescue of people who have got into difficulties grows. People lose their oars and are left drifting helplessly. Gales spring up suddenly and yachts can lose their sails or their rudders, or they can capsize without proper control.

Then there is the other danger of water-wings, rubber life-belts and inflatable rubber mattresses. Bathers rarely know anything about the current on the beaches where they swim, and during the summer many people are carried away, floating helplessly on these things. Rubber belts and water-wings are said to be an aid to learning to swim. In fact they are not, for a person using them is apt to become lazy, to place too much reliance on them, and not bother to learn to swim properly. It is these people who can cause trouble if a current or tide carries them away from a beach. There is no substitute for learning to swim through one's own efforts. Anything else is a hindrance.

It is an unpleasant experience being drawn out to sea on a rubber float, seeing the shore receding and being unable to get back. If someone sees the person drifting away the alarm can be raised quickly. But a rubber float with a single person on it is a very small thing on the sea, and often no one knows anything has happened until the person is missed, per-haps hours later. By the time the alarm goes out the person on the float may have become so cold that he or she has fallen off. If they are lucky the life-boat reaches them before that happens.

But the launching of the life-boat at any time costs money, and while the Institution in no way grudges the use of its fleet for this purpose its funds are not unlimited, and going in search of a missing bather or pleasure-bent amateur sailor can detract from some bigger service which might be necessary. It is particu-larly irritating when in many cases the whole thing might have been avoided with a little more care and forethought from the person they rescue.

Of course not all such rescues are the result of stupidity or carelessness, but if there were some official way of judging the competence of people going pleasure cruising before they are allowed to leave harbour, and if bathers would learn to swim properly and not trust their lives to rubber floats and water-wings, the work of the life-boats would be considerably lessened.

Sometimes, however, even the most competent yachtsmen can be taken unawares by sudden freak changes in the weather or by some unforeseeable accident to their sails, engines or steering gear.

Unpredictable weather changes are always a source of annoyance to holiday makers, but little more. To the life-boatmen they may mean a lot of extra work.

The life-boathouse at Selsey is reached by a gangway set on stilt-like legs leading out over the shelving, shingly beach. This is a new boathouse, built only a few years ago. The old one stood a little further to the east and the gangway leading to it was even longer. Inside the new boathouse the life-boat *Canadian Pacific* lies, its bows facing the doors which lead on to the slipway and so down into the sea. The life-boat station is situated almost at the point of Selsey Bill, guarding the eastern approaches to the Solent and the big naval base at Portsmouth.

During the summer yachts and pleasure cruisers of all types can be seen all round Selsey, and it is craft of this kind that the Selsey life-boat is often called out to help.

On 28 and 29 July 1956 freak gales struck the entire coast of Great Britain. Coming unexpectedly as they did at the height of the yachting season, life-boats of the R.N.L.I. were launched on a record number of services. In a hectic day and night there were fifty-two launches all round the coast involving forty life-boat stations, and 107 lives were saved. During no other similar twenty-four-hour period has the R.N.L.I. been so busy.

At Selsey on 29 July conditions were appalling. The sea was not running high, but it was boiling: a seething mass of tortured water flinging spray so high that visibility was reduced at times almost to nil. Wind velocity reached ninety miles an hour and some members of the crew believe that it even topped the hundred mark on one or two occasions.

It was in such conditions that the coastguard at Chichester Harbour observed a yacht flying distress signals heading in the direction of West Wittering. The coastguard rang the Selsey coastguard who immediately got in touch with the honorary secretary of the Selsey life-boat station.

The crew were summoned by the maroons. Most of them are fishermen, and so live fairly near the station, so they heard the summons which they could easily have missed in the gale. But of course they were waiting for this call. In the conditions it

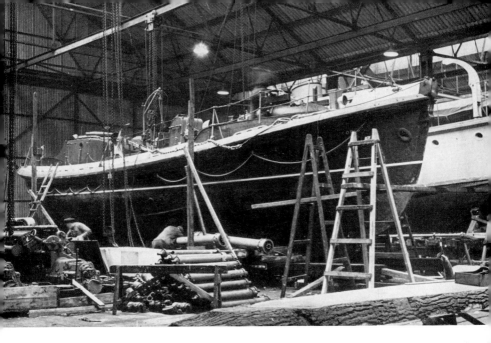

A life-boat nearing completion at J. Samuel White's boatyard at Cowes

A stage in the building of a modern life-boat at Osborne's boatyard in Littlehampton

Shortly before this photograph was taken the *Hindlea's* crew of eight were taken off by the Moelfre lifeboat.

See chapter xv

would have been amazing if it had not come, and they were
ready to go.

But being ready to go and actually going were two different
things. To reach the life-boathouse the crew had to make their
way along the exposed gangway, and the force of the wind was
so strong that they had to pull themselves along by the railings
hand over hand.

Sixteen minutes after the call came the life-boat was launched.
Mr. J. R. B. Harries, the present honorary secretary of the
Selsey station, told me that many people in the boathouse that
day gave the life-boat only a fifty-fifty chance of coming back.
Yet much later, when I returned from going out on exercise in
the life-boat with the crew, many of whom had served on that
day, I asked them what conditions had been like. There was a
thoughtful, almost embarrassed silence. Then one man removed
his pipe from his mouth, examined the tobacco in the bowl
critically, and said:

'Well, it was a bit rough.'

The others nodded agreement, and it was impossible to make
them say more.

Almost immediately on leaving her station something happened
which made the life-boat's chances of success even more remote.

Lobster fishing is one of the local occupations at Selsey, and
lobster pots had been put down at sea before the gale sprang up.
Now with the force of the wind and the turbulent water many
of these had broken adrift, and almost as soon as the life-boat
left the boathouse some of these lines fouled her propellers and
a cork float jammed in her rudder. It was impossible in the
conditions to stop the life-boat and clear the lines. Had they
done so the life-boat would certainly have been swamped. With
steering difficult and engine power cut almost by half the life-
boat made her way slowly round Selsey Bill in search of the yacht.

Nobody knows the name of the yacht or what happened to
her. But the Selsey life-boat never found her.

In those conditions it was not surprising, but the life-boat's
journey was not in vain.

A reef of submerged rocks runs out eastward from the shore
to the west of Selsey. Twenty minutes after leaving her station
the life-boat sighted a vessel in distress near this reef.

She was a forty-ton Dutch yacht called the *Maaslust*, a beautiful ship, but not very beautiful at that moment. Her sails had blown away. She had an engine, but this was doing no good. The seas were breaking steeply round her and she was yawing wildly. Coxswain Douglas Grant took the life-boat alongside her, but as he did so a huge sea made the *Maaslust* sheer away, and the coxswain decided to try again.

As he was about to do so the weather cleared for a moment and in the break another yacht was seen close by in even worse difficulties than the *Maaslust*. Her sails too had been blown away and her rigging was trailing in a tangled mess in the water. The life-boat crew could see people on the deck of the yacht. She had an anchor out, but she was in a very dangerous position near the same reef.

It seemed to Coxswain Grant that this yacht, the *Bloodhound*, was in an even worse plight than the *Maaslust*, so he decided to take her crew off first. Despite the restrictions on the life-boat's engines he brought her up on the starboard side and held her bows against the *Bloodhound*. Within a few minutes seven men and two women were taken off, and the life-boat returned to the *Maaslust*.

The *Maaslust* had leeboards which made it impossible to bring the life-boat alongside to take off her crew. There were six people aboard her: three men, a woman and two children— a girl of about ten and a baby in arms. With a child so young it was essential that no risks be taken. The life-boat had somehow to get close in. Coxswain Grant took the life-boat away from the *Maaslust* and then turned and drove head on into her, ramming the bows of the life-boat hard into the *Maaslust*'s side, and while the two boats lay locked together and tossing in the heavy sea he held her in position with the engines, giving the two mechanics orders to go ahead, stop, or go astern as the state of the sea made it necessary. All those on board the *Maaslust* had life-lines attached to them, but these had become entangled with the yacht's rigging. The life-boat crew would have to cut these lines before those on the *Maaslust* could be transferred, because if some particularly heavy sea caused the life-boat to sheer away the people held by the life-lines would be dragged off the life-boat before the lines were cut, and if this happened to the baby he could have been drowned before the life-boat had a chance to bring him in again.

The baby was quite calm. He only began to cry when he saw one of the life-boat crew produce a knife to cut the life-line round him. But the line had to be cut.

Within a few minutes the six people were taken off. They were given blankets and taken to the shelter of the cabin. The baby was quite calm again. A few minutes later the *Maaslust* disappeared. She was never seen again, nor was any trace of wreckage ever found. With her engine still running she vanished into the sea as though she had never existed. Even the dinghy she had been towing disappeared.

By now the life-boat was in difficulties herself. Her stem was damaged, the rudder had jammed completely, perhaps with more lines from the wreck of the *Maaslust*, and with her engines only working at half power it seemed as though she herself would fall a victim of the rocks from which she had saved the crews of the *Maaslust* and the *Bloodhound*. The only thing which might prevent the life-boat drifting on to the rocks and being smashed to matchwood was to lower the anchor and hope it held them off long enough to get some use out of the rudder again. The coxswain was about to give the order to lower the anchor when the rudder suddenly freed itself.

Coxswain Grant decided to take his fifteen survivors to Portsmouth and he set a course that way. Visibility was still very bad, and they had hardly started for Portsmouth when another yacht was sighted crossing the life-boat's bows just ahead. She was almost on her beam ends and would clearly sink in a very short time.

She was the *Coima*, and she had been lying in the sheltered anchorage of St Helen's Roads off the Isle of Wight and had been blown from there by the fury of the gale. She had a crew of three, and when they were first seen they were sitting in the yacht with their heads lowered, having given up all hope. They were in fact simply waiting to be drowned. They had pumped and baled to get the water out of the *Coima*, but the sea had been too much for them. Now, exhausted and without hope, they were waiting for the end.

The arrival of the life-boat was providential. If the life-boat's rudder had not freed itself exactly when it did the two boats could have passed without even knowing of each other's existence. The three of the crew were taken off and the yacht sank almost immediately. Parts of her were later washed up on the shore.

Coxswain Grant took the life-boat astern, and as he did so some of the lines fouling the propellers were thrown clear and engine power was increased.

The eighteen survivors were now crowded in the cabin with blankets, and the life-boat sailed for Portsmouth. She reached the harbour at a quarter to five and landed the survivors. The life-boat crew were given dry clothes and food, and then returned with the life-boat to Selsey. By now the gale had moderated a little, and on her way home the life-boat sighted another yacht, but she was under control and did not need help.

The life-boat returned to her station at ten o'clock, having been out on service for nearly ten hours. She had gone out to help a yacht which she never found, and instead she had saved the crews of three others.

Coxswain Douglas Grant was awarded the silver medal for these rescues.

The following day the life-boat was launched again and made for the *Bloodhound* which was still riding to her anchor, and towed her into Portsmouth. She was the only vessel of the three which was still afloat.

A little while afterwards the *Bloodhound* was bought for a new owner—Her Majesty the Queen.

CHAPTER THIRTEEN

St Ives—1958

So far we have seen something of the life-boat's work at sea, but there is another aspect of the service which in many ways is more dangerous even than that, and that is rescuing people from the shore.

People occasionally get trapped on ledges of sea cliffs, or cut off by the tide on beaches, and if rescue from the land is impossible, only the life-boat can help. This usually involves coming close in to the shore, often amongst dangerous rocks and strong currents and tides, and it is the life-boat, with its great manœuvrability and shallow draft, which is sent in to take them off.

Generally such rescues are performed in reasonable weather conditions, for people do not as a rule go for walks along exposed stretches of the shore or climb steep cliffs in howling gales and pouring rain. If the weather should happen to be bad, such rescues can be amongst the most dangerous the life-boatmen are asked to carry out.

A few miles south of Bamburgh, where the first life-boat station in the world was founded, lies North Sunderland. There is no life-boat station at Bamburgh now. It was closed as long ago as 1898, and now North Sunderland undertakes the work which the Bamburgh life-boat did in the old days. The life-boat is stationed at the adjoining village of Seahouses, for North Sunderland itself lies a mile or so inland.

Two miles north of North Sunderland lies the scattering of the Farne Islands where Grace Darling and her father rescued the survivors of the *Forfarshire* a century and a quarter ago. In fact, the North Sunderland life-boat is named *Grace Darling* in memory of her.

It was near the inner Farne Island that the coastguard saw, on the afternoon of 12 July 1959, a single man in a canoe close

under the western shore. It was a fine but blustery day. The
sea was not too rough, but near the island a heavy ground sea
was running. It was an hour after low water.

Clearly the canoe was in a dangerous position, and the coastguard told the honorary secretary of the North Sunderland life-
boat station. Ten minutes after the canoe was first sighted the
life-boat carriage was pushed into the sea by its tractor, the
Grace Darling slipped off the carriage and began her two-mile
journey to the island.

By the time the life-boat reached the island the crew could
see that the man in the canoe had indeed got into difficulties.
There was no sign of the canoe, but the man himself was hanging on to a ledge of a seventy-foot-high cliff at the south-west
corner of the island. The ledge was about twelve feet above the
water and the sea was breaking round his feet. The tide was
coming in. His canoe had capsized in the confused water at the
base of the cliff and he had managed to reach this position—
one of considerable danger.

Coxswain Thomas Dawson realized that taking the man off
was not going to be easy. He was hanging from the ledge with
both hands, so the line-throwing gun would be useless. He would
have no free hand to grab the line as it came over. Somehow
the coxswain would have to get the man into the life-boat without using a line. Clearly someone would have to swim from the
life-boat to the cliff to take the man off.

Not one member of the life-boat crew could swim.

There is nothing unusual about this amongst fishermen who
form the bulk of the life-boats' crews. Many of them cannot
swim, and even the founder of the Institution, Sir William
Hillary, who helped to rescue more than three hundred lives
while he served with the Douglas crew, could not swim a stroke.

But every member of the crew volunteered to take a line
across to the man. Coxswain Dawson knew that to undertake
a journey of that nature would be extremely dangerous for anyone unable to swim, and he could not ask any of his men to do
it. He decided to take the line himself.

The life-boat was anchored as close to the shore as it safely
could be. The wind was blowing on to the shore and the ground
sea was rising sometimes to a height of twelve feet. When the

anchor was holding firmly the life-boat was allowed to drop down towards the cliff on its cable until the stern was sixty feet from the shore.

Coxswain Dawson handed over command of the life-boat to Second Coxswain Walker.

A line was attached to Coxswain Dawson's life-jacket and he lowered himself over the side. While the second coxswain held the life-boat in position by manœuvring the engines to give Coxswain Dawson enough slack line, the coxswain made his way with great difficulty through the choppy, broken water to the base of the cliff.

Coxswain Dawson reached the man on the cliff and found that he too could not swim, so he signalled to the life-boat for another life-jacket. This was attached to the line and Coxswain Dawson pulled it to the shore. He put it on the man and then managed to lower him to a ledge nearer the water, from where he was pulled back to the life-boat. Then the coxswain himself was dragged back by the line which he had brought across with him. Both men were hauled through heavy, broken water, but though both were bruised, neither was injured.

The life-boat returned to her station, having been away for less than an hour and a half. Coxswain Dawson was awarded the bronze medal for this rescue.

A slightly more complicated rescue of the same type had taken place almost a year before.

Hellsmouth lies on the north Cornwall coast, a mile or two from Godrevy Head which is the eastern tip of St Ives Bay. Here massive cliffs tower out of the sea, sheer and stern and forbidding. From the top the sea is far below and huge rocks look like pebbles. The cliff face is full of caves and coves, and on the top are the remains of old tin mine workings. The whole area is riddled with tunnels and passages and deep holes and shafts which are a delight and a danger to the visitors.

On 9 August 1958 a party of five people set out to explore one of the most famous of these caves, Smuggler's Cave. The party consisted of two men, two girls, one aged eighteen and the other twelve, and a boy of fourteen. They took a rope with them. It was to be a grand holiday adventure.

At the top of the cliff they made their way along a tunnel for about a hundred yards and then reached an opening which led downwards to the cave beneath. Here they secured the rope and one after the other they climbed down it, thirty-five feet into the dark mysteriousness of the cave. The sea was booming and reverberating at the entrance and they spent twenty minutes exploring the cave before the cold and mustiness dampened their enthusiasm and they decided to return.

They got back to the place where their rope hung down from the hole in the roof of the cave, and one of the men began to climb up first. But in the interval the rope had become damp and greasy from the atmosphere in the cave, and half-way up the rope he lost his grip and fell, injuring his head on the rocks beneath.

Suddenly the adventure became a lot more serious than it had been before. Even if the other members of the party had felt they could risk climbing the greasy rope, they now had an injured man to take with them, and exit that way was clearly impossible. At the mouth of the cave the sea was surging, creeping steadily inwards, for the tide was rising.

At a quarter to six in the evening the other man of the party realized that he would have to try to get help. The only way he could do this was by swimming out of the cave and trying to climb the cliff face to the heights. This would be no easy job. It also meant leaving the two girls and the boy to look after the injured man, but it was the only thing to do, and he set out on his journey. Fortunately for them all he managed it and reached the top of the cliff in an exhausted state. On the road which runs along the top stands a little café where summer visitors to Hellsmouth can buy sweets and ice cream, and the man managed to reach this and blurt out his urgent message.

At twenty-five minutes to seven the St Ives police contacted the honorary secretary of the St Ives life-boat station and told him what had happened. Eleven minutes later the 35½-foot Liverpool-type life-boat *Edgar, George, Orlando and Eva Child* was launched into St Ives harbour from her tractor, and Coxswain Daniel Roach set a course for Smuggler's Cave. He took a dinghy in tow.

The weather was overcast and drizzling and there was a slight sea mist, but the sea was calm and there was no wind. Conditions were much the same the day I stood in the boathouse with Coxswain Roach, leaning on the launching tractor facing the harbour. Coxswain Roach pointed towards the sea.

'You wouldn't think you'd have much trouble out there, would you?' he said. 'It just shows, you can never be sure.'

The life-boat reached the entrance to Smuggler's Cave at 7.25. Here there was a fairly heavy ground sea running, and Coxswain Roach immediately sent the dinghy into the cave with four members of the life-boat's crew, one of them being his own son.

What Coxswain Roach did not know and could not know was that the ground sea was heavier inside the cave than it was outside, and the crew of the dinghy found the going a lot more difficult than they had anticipated, partly because of the ground sea and partly because of the rocky bottom. When the dinghy was thirty yards inside the cave it was holed by a rock and sank. The four members of the life-boat's crew swam and waded another seventy yards until they reached the head of the cave and there they found the injured man with the two girls and the boy. But now the situation had changed. Instead of four people to be rescued from the cave there were now eight, and the coxswain of the life-boat could have no knowledge of what had happened to the dinghy. Clearly he must be told what the situation was. The noise inside the cave, with the surging sea echoing and re-echoing round the rocky walls, made shouting useless. The life-boat signalman, Daniel Paynter, who was one of those who had been in the dinghy, realized that he would have to swim out of the cave and reach the life-boat, and he set out to do this.

The tide was flooding fast now, and in addition the ground sea made his job extremely arduous. By the time he had swum clear of the cave entrance he had reached the limit of his endurance, but the coxswain saw him appear and steered the life-boat in towards him and threw him a line. But Signalman Paynter was now too weak even to grasp it, so Motor Mechanic Michael Peters jumped overboard with the line, swam to Signalman Paynter and secured the line round him. The two men were pulled back aboard, a back-breaking job for the only two men left aboard the life-boat.

Now Coxswain Roach was in difficulties. He had no dinghy left with which to enter the cave, there were seven people trapped inside and the tide was still coming in . . .

Motor Mechanic Peters volunteered to swim into the cave with a line. The line gun could not be used in these circumstances, for the inside of the cave was dark and those in the life-boat could not see where to fire it, so two gun lines were joined together and Motor Mechanic Peters jumped overboard once more and swam into the cave. It should have been easier swimming in than it had been for Signalman Paynter swimming out, for the tide helped to carry him in, but he had a line attached to his life-jacket and the longer the stretch of line between him and the life-boat the more the sea dragged it. Also he took a breeches buoy and two spare life-jackets with him, and these hampered his movements considerably.

Coxswain Roach watched the bobbing head disappear into the gloom of the cave mouth and realized that he must give Motor Mechanic Peters as much line as possible, so he anchored the life-boat in the mouth of the cave, and kept her bows headed towards the sea by constant manœuvring of his engines.

Motor Mechanic Peters waded ashore with his load, and took charge. A heavier line was pulled into the cave from the life-boat by the light line, and once they had this the people in the cave were all tied to it, one behind the other. The injured man was put into the breeches buoy, the two girls were given the two life-jackets which Motor Mechanic Peters had brought with him, and the boy was secured to Martin Roach, the coxswain's son.

Then Motor Mechanic Peters hauled himself out along the line to a place where he could see the coxswain, and gave the order to heave. The men on the life-boat began to pull the line in and as they did so the strange procession entered the water and began to make its way out of the cave. Motor Mechanic Peters kept the line clear of the rocks in the cave until he was sure that everyone was safely on their way, and then he pulled himself ahead along the line to the life-boat and climbed aboard to lend a hand pulling the line and helping the rescued people aboard as they reached the life-boat.

All seven were safely taken aboard. At five minutes past nine

the life-boat weighed anchor and forty minutes later reached
St Ives harbour. What had started out as a foolhardy escapade
had been saved from becoming tragedy in the nick of time.

Motor Mechanic Michael Peters was awarded the silver medal
for his part in the rescue, and Coxswain Daniel Roach and
Signalman Daniel Paynter were each awarded the bronze medal.

CHAPTER FOURTEEN

Lerwick—1958

A life-boat is the supreme example of the shipwright's craft. It has to be, for it endures worse conditions and meets them more often than any other kind of vessel afloat. Some are built at Messrs. William Osborne's yard at Littlehampton, but most of the modern life-boats are built at Cowes on the Isle of Wight by Messrs. Samuel White or by Messrs. Groves and Guttridge. In the midst of this great yachting centre, both these firms have had long experience in building life-boats, and in fact White's have been building them for the Institution for over a hundred years. The first life-boat they built cost £116—a three-hundredth part of what the cheapest life-boat costs today.

From the very beginning life-boats were built of wood, and this is still the case today. At the time of the steam life-boats the hulls were built of steel because of the immense weight of these boats, but it was found that steel was too unyielding and brittle for successful life-boat work. Many years of experiment have gone into present-day life-boats and they are built to the most exact and rigid standards, for on the craftsmanship in the boat depends the lives of the crews and the lives of the countless people the crew will have to rescue.

Different types of wood are used for building a life-boat. Teak from Burma, mahogany from Africa, English oak and Western red cedar are all used for different parts of the life-boat. The framework of the boat is almost all built of oak, while the keel is made from teak or mahogany. The planking is laid diagonally across the sides, unlike the method used in most other wooden boatbuilding, and is double skinned—in other words two layers of planking are used—for added toughness and endurance. The planks are of mahogany or teak, the toughest, hardest wood there is. Below the decks flotation cases are fitted. These are made of pine, chemically treated, painted, and covered in canvas. Each case is tested by placing it in a tank and submerging it to make sure it is absolutely watertight. These flotation cases are fitted in every possible vacant space below the deck, and serve an essential purpose in the life-boat. Not only do they increase her buoyancy, but should the life-boat be holed below the waterline the extent to which the water enters is limited to the number of cases breached, so that the modern life-boat is as near the life-boatman's age-old dream of being unsinkable as it could be. All fittings are of copper or brass.

All life-boats built nowadays have two diesel engines of up to sixty horse power each. The engine room is a watertight compartment on its own, and each engine is enclosed in a watertight casing, so that the engines will continue to work even if they are under water.

The larger life-boats are equipped with cabins, and even the smallest have protection for the coxswain while he stands at the wheel, and a canopy under which the motor mechanics can work at the controls and use the radio-telephone in comparative comfort, while at the same time being close to the coxswain so that he can shout orders directly to them.

Every life-boat has the best and most efficient compass obtainable, for on the compass depends the boat's safety and her ability to reach a casualty quickly. The compass must read accurately at all times, even when the life-boat is to all intents and purposes looping the loop.

Radio-telephone, VHF radio for direct communication between the life-boat and aircraft which may be assisting in a search, loud-hailer, searchlight, breeches buoy and line-gun, stretcher, first-aid kit and a hundred and one other essential pieces of equipment are installed in the life-boat, and now echo-sounding equipment is going into life-boats as they go for overhauls. This is a development of the wartime asdic, which enabled ships on the surface to locate the presence of submarines by a system of shock waves sent from the bottom of the ship to the sea bed and back again. Anything coming between the ship and the sea bottom bounced the wave back more quickly. Nowadays this invention is used for more peaceful purposes. Fishing boats use it to locate shoals of fish; and life-boats are **not** concerned with the presence of submarines, but the echo-sounding equipment will tell the coxswain all the time exactly how much water he has under him, most important information when working amongst sandbanks or on a rocky coast.

At the moment life-boats are not equipped with radar, and many people wonder why this most important aid should be missing. The reason is that a life-boat's aerial on top of the mast is not high enough, and in normal working conditions the life-boat pitches and tosses to such an extent that radar has been found to be of little use. However, this situation is already changing. The new Oakley 48½-foot self-righting life-boat is the first to be fitted with radar apparatus.

The old problem of wreckage fouling propellers has been at least partially solved not only by housing the propellers in tunnels, but by building hatches in the deck of the life-boat directly over the propeller shafts. Should wreckage become entangled in the propellers the hatches can be removed and the wreckage cut away from the deck.

One of the points raised in the Duke of Northumberland's competition in 1851 was the fact that life-boats at that time did not free themselves of water fast enough. It often happens that the sea sweeps right over the life-boat and it is important that this water should drain away as fast as possible. One or two of the models submitted for the competition had curious answers to this criticism, mostly with holes bored through the bottom of the boat to let the water drain away. There seems to have been little thought on the part of the designers about how to keep the water from coming in. One of the models submitted contained no less than 3,600 holes for this purpose.

Modern life-boats have valves let into the side of the boat just above a watertight deck, which is itself some distance above the waterline. Water will pour out through these valves, but cannot pour in. A modern life-boat will empty itself of water within a matter of five or six seconds.

No one maintains that the modern life-boats are the last word in design. Designs are ever-changing and experiments go on endlessly to increase the capabilities of the boats and to make them even safer for the crews who sail in them. Within a few years there may well be some new and revolutionary ideas for improving life-boats, and if such an event were to take place the R.N.L.I. would be the first to welcome it with open arms.

It may take anything up to two years to build a life-boat, for every step is closely watched and carefully scrutinized. When she is finished the boat is painted in the Institution's famous livery of red, blue and white, and she undergoes exhaustive trials before she is passed as fit for service. The crew from the station to which the life-boat is assigned come to the yard to take charge of her, and they sail her from the yard to the station, which may be a distance of several hundred miles. During this journey the worse weather she meets the better, for it gives her crew the chance to see how their new boat handles.

A service of dedication and a naming ceremony is held at the station when the new life-boat reaches it, always a moving occasion, with the life-boat fresh in its new paint, decked with flags and bunting, other boats in the harbour also flying flags in celebration, some famous person naming the life-boat, and the enormous crowds which always gather to see the new boat. Then the life-boat is ready, after many months of preparation, to go to the rescue wherever it may be necessary and from whomever the call may come.

There is a fellowship among fishermen the world over which breaks down barriers of language and belief. Perhaps it is the common dangers faced by those who earn their living from the sea which causes this deep understanding. The crew of the Lerwick life-boat are all fishermen, and the sea round Shetland is the fishing ground for many nations.

The 16 October 1958 was a bad day for both weather and for the fishing at Lerwick. Coxswain John Sales of Lerwick had been out fishing all day and returned home with little to show for it. He was looking forward to getting to bed and having a well-earned rest. There was a gale blowing from the north and the sea was very rough. A warm, comfortable bed was an inviting thought at such a time, and Coxswain Sales was in fact about to retire for the night when his telephone rang. It was nine o'clock. A telephone call at that time of night could mean only one thing.

It was the honorary secretary of the life-boat station to say that he had received a message that a Russian trawler was in difficulties and needed assistance. Coxswain Sales asked for the position of the trawler and was told it was off the Holm of Skaw. This was disturbing news, for the Holm of Skaw is a rocky, uninhabited islet off the north of Unst, the most northerly of the Shetland Islands, and fifty miles north of Lerwick.

This was all the information available at the moment, but it was enough to go on. Shortly after half past nine the new 52-foot Barnett life-boat *Claude Cecil Staniforth* slipped her moorings in Lerwick harbour and headed out to sea on her first service.

It was a pitch-black night with squally showers of rain, and the life-boat had to head straight into the teeth of the gale for the entire journey. The seas swept down on her from directly ahead, filling the life-boat again and again. As they battered their way northwards a radio-telephone message came through with more information. The trawler had struck the Holm of Skaw and had sunk, but there were clearly some survivors, for people on the shore of Unst could hear men shouting from the islet. The local life-saving team and twenty men from the R.A.F. station at Saxa Vord were on the spot, but conditions were too bad for them to reach the survivors and the life-boat's help was urgently required. Three trawlers and a Shackleton aircraft were also taking part in the search.

Coxswain Sales held a quick conference with his crew, shouting to make his voice heard above the roar of the waves and the wind, frequently stopped by the seas pouring into the life-boat. The Holm of Skaw was a long way away, and neither the coxswain nor any member of the crew felt that they knew enough about conditions on that coast to affect a rescue in the darkness.

Then a further radio-telephone message crackled through to the life-boat. A local man, Mr Duncan Mouat, who lived at Baltasound on Unst, who was an experienced yachtsman and knew the coastline well, had volunteered to act as pilot to the life-boat. Coxswain Sales decided to accept this offer, and at about three o'clock in the morning he brought the life-boat in to Haroldswick on Unst and picked up Mr Mouat. Then they set out northwards again for the Holm of Skaw. The weather

The *Argo Delos* aground on Torr Beg islet. The Portrush life-boat is returning to her after clearing ropes fouling her propeller. See chapter XVI

A man being rescued from the shore in a breeches buoy. The St Ives life-boat is standing by

was showing no signs of improving—the gale was still blowing fiercely, direct from the Arctic Circle.

When they were only about three miles away from the islet one of the life-boat's engines stopped. In that sea they could not stop to investigate, so they proceeded on one engine, and under Mr Mouat's direction they approached the Holm of Skaw.

Coxswain Sales switched on the searchlight and the white beam stabbed through the darkness, spray and rain. In the beam they saw the islet, the wicked line of rocks and the white foam breaking over them. They saw more, for in the search-light's glare they saw three men clinging to the rocks, waving frantically towards them.

They stopped the engine and dropped anchor. The breeches buoy was prepared, and while some of the crew made ready to take the men off the islet, three others set about finding out what had happened to the stalled engine. This did not take long. Through the hatch in the deck they could see a mass of line and cork floats wound round the propeller shaft. They had picked up a fishing net, probably from the wrecked trawler. After a lot of pulling and cutting they managed to free the propeller and the engine was restarted.

Meanwhile Coxwain Sales moved the searchlight beam to show the men on the islet where the line was going to be fired. The second coxswain fired it exactly to the right position and it was caught by one of the survivors. There was nowhere on the islet where the block for the line could be attached, so one of the men held it while two others were brought across in the breeches buoy. Then the third man—he was the captain of the wrecked trawler—was dragged over himself. One by one the three men were pulled aboard the life-boat. They were in a dreadful state—almost naked, cold, soaked and thoroughly ex-hausted. They were taken into the cabin, rubbed down briskly to restore their circulation, given hot soup and wrapped up in blankets. Only the captain could speak a very little English, so it was difficult to communicate with them, but the coxswain understood from the captain that there was still another man left on the Holm of Skaw and he had a broken leg.

Conditions were still very bad, and Coxswain Sales decided it was too dangerous to risk taking the life-boat any closer to the islet and he formed another plan. Already there were three trawlers and an aircraft searching the sea for further survivors, so the rescue of any men from the water round about could safely be left to them. If there was a man with a broken leg left on those rocks the life-boat would have to land someone on the Holm of Skaw to bring him off.

So Coxswain Sales took the life-boat to Norwick about two miles south to pick up a small boat. It was now nearly half past five in the morning. They took a small boat on board the life-boat and returned to the islet. There they launched the small boat, and Mr Mouat and three of the life-boat's crew took her in and carried out a thorough search, but they found no one there. If in fact there had been anyone left on the Holm of Skaw he must have been washed out to sea. Later a body was washed ashore at Lambaness a little to the south, and it is possible that this was the man the captain meant. The small boat was taken back on board and the life-boat began to search a wider area.

At half past seven they sighted the wrecked trawler. She was the *Urbe*, and all that could be seen of her was part of her bow and her masts. Clearly no one could be left alive aboard her. The coxswain declared that he was amazed that three men could have made their way from the wreck to the Holm of Skaw in any case, and said they must have been very hardy to have withstood the extreme cold.

Coxswain Sales decided to return to Baltasound to land Mr Mouat, but before he could do so another radio-telephone message came through to say that an aircraft was going to join the search now that it was light, and the life-boat was asked to stand by to keep in contact with it.

The search went on for another four and a half hours, but no further survivors were found. The search was abandoned and the life-boat turned at last for Baltasound. There they landed Mr Mouat, and the three Russians were taken to the local hotel and given clothes, and they and the life-boat crew had a good hot meal.

The *Urbe* was one of the trawlers in a Russian fishing fleet and during the search the parent ship *Tomsk* had repeatedly asked that the survivors should be taken to her immediately, but it was decided that it would be too dangerous to try to transfer the rescued men in that weather.

After the life-boat crew and the Russian survivors had been fed, they set out once again to return to Lerwick. By now they had taken on board two bodies which had been recovered by other vessels taking part in the search, and these bodies and the three survivors were all that was left out of a total crew of twenty-five.

It was nearly a quarter to three in the afternoon, and half an hour later the coxswain was instructed to return to Baltasound and land the survivors for repatriation to the *Tomsk*.

Back at Baltasound a Russian launch was waiting to take the survivors and the bodies back to the *Tomsk*. The three Russians shook hands with the life-boat crew and thanked them in halting English, and then they were taken aboard the launch and set out for the parent ship.

The life-boat returned to Lerwick, arriving there at ten past nine in the evening, having been out on service for very nearly forty-eight hours, during which time they had fought heavy seas and biting cold, had no sleep and only one good meal.

Coxswain Sales was awarded the silver medal and Mr Duncan Mouat the bronze medal, and Moscow radio paid tribute to the work of the Lerwick life-boat, referring to the crew's 'brilliant skill, vast courage and selfless heroism in fighting a treacherous sea'.

CHAPTER FIFTEEN

Moelfre—1959

The R.N.L.I.'s boatbuilding programme is not made up entirely of building new life-boats. Not unnaturally life-boats are frequently damaged when they are out on service, and repairs are necessary. Sometimes the damage is so severe that the life-boat may be out of commission for weeks, even months, and has to be returned to the boatbuilder's yard. This constant repair work is an endless but unavoidable strain on the Institution's resources. Minor repairs can usually be carried out at the life-boat's station, but the major repairs mean the life-boat's disappearance for quite a long time.

On the Great North Road at Boreham Wood in Hertfordshire stands the R.N.L.I.'s depot. This building was opened in 1939 and here are stored the thousands of spare parts which every day are sent out to stations all over the country. Work goes on round the clock here, and everything from an anchor to an oilskin, from a rope to a radio set is stored ready to be despatched whenever it is needed.

Besides having to be sent away from her station if she is badly damaged, all life-boats must from time to time be serviced and overhauled thoroughly, and such an overhaul at the yards takes time.

The R.N.L.I. keeps a reserve fleet of boats for these occasions. This fleet consists of older boats which have been withdrawn from active service but which are still perfectly seaworthy and competent to perform the most arduous duties. There are roughly twenty-five boats in this fleet at any time, and they are of all different types. This is necessary, because to replace the small life-boat at, say, St Abbs in Berwickshire with a 52-foot Barnett life-boat would be pointless. The boat at St Abbs is launched down a slipway into the harbour, and at low water the harbour at St Abbs is so shallow that only a $35\frac{1}{2}$-foot life-boat can be launched into it. Similarly to replace the 52-foot Barnett life-boat at Lerwick with a small Oakley self-righter which has less than half the operational range, would not give anything like adequate coverage for the station.

One of the main difficulties about replacing a life-boat with a temporary reserve boat is that the crew at the station must get used to the replacement. Crews become familiar with their own boats through constant usage. They know exactly how she will handle in different circumstances, and it is not just a question of getting into a strange boat and setting off. The coxswain and crew must know exactly what their new charge is going to do and what she is capable of.

Normally the crew like to have an exercise in their reserve boat before a service is required, but sometimes this is not possible.

One of the most striking examples of this happened in Anglesey.

Coxswain Richard Evans stuck his hands in the pockets of his reefer jacket and his eyes sparkled with humour. Somehow one imagines that all coxswains must have voices like parade-ground sergeant majors, but I have not found this to be so. All the coxswains I have spoken to have quiet voices and they are sparing with words. This is far more effective and impressive than any long harangue or loud-mouth roaring. Coxswain Evans is no exception.

'We thought we had the worst boat in the whole fleet,' he said.

I looked startled and glanced at the beautiful, gleaming white, blue and red hull and stern of the Moelfre life-boat *Watkin Williams* behind him in the boathouse. He followed my glance and laughed.

'No, not that one. We had a reserve boat at the time. She was a mess—that's what we all thought.'

Motor Mechanic Evan Owens grinned and nodded agreement. They were clearly enjoying a private joke, and I settled down to hear what it was all about.

The coxswain and crew of the Moelfre life-boat station were disgusted with their boat—not with their own boat, which in October 1959 had gone for a refit, but with the reserve life-boat which they had been sent in its place. This was a 41-foot Watson-type life-boat built over twenty years before, and for years she had been kept afloat, lately at New Brighton in Cheshire. A life-boat lying afloat suffers more from the action of sea and weather than one which is housed in a boathouse ashore. Its hull is not the gleaming white of a shore-based boat. It is painted a dull green for anti-fouling purposes, its brass-work is apt to become badly tarnished by the salt water, and the *Edmund and Mary Robinson* was no exception. She looked very different from the Moelfre life-boat in which the crew, as with all life-boat crews, took such a great pride, hosing her down with fresh water on her return from service to wash away the corrosive salt. This is done at all life-boat stations, but it seemed pointless to hose down this reserve boat. She lacked the gleaming white hull, the bright red and blue paintwork above, and the shining brass. Altogether, as Coxswain Evans said, she looked a mess.

Furthermore they had had no chance to try her out yet, and Coxswain Evans was hoping against hope that they would never be called out on service in her, because he was sure she would prove herself obstinate and unseaworthy.

But his hopes did not live long. Very soon after the reserve life-boat reached the station at Moelfre a south-westerly gale sprang up. Soon it veered to the north, and Coxswain Evans knew that this spelt trouble. Wind from the north always meant trouble.

Moelfre lies on the east coast of Anglesey, a quiet little village huddled at the edge of the sea, a backwater where nothing seems to happen. But when the wind blows from the north and the sea springs into a raging inferno there is little peace here. Since the life-boat station was established at Moelfre more than a hundred and thirty years ago the life-boat has saved well over six hundred lives.

Lying almost due west of Liverpool and the busy river Mersey, Moelfre is in the path of many shipping lanes, and on 27 October, when the northerly gale was at its height, a message came from the coastguard at Moelfre to say that a small vessel riding out the gale in the doubtful shelter of Dulas Bay just to the north of the village was dragging her anchor.

Coxswain Evans knew what that meant. The vessel would run before the gale and be dashed to pieces on the rocks, almost within sight of the life-boat station unless action was taken immediately

He left his house in the full knowledge that he had not time to summon his crew. It is difficult, if not impossible, in a small place like Moelfre to form a crew who are permanently within call. Some of the crew were engaged on roadworks a good many miles away from Moelfre and could never get to the life-boat station in time. He could not afford to wait while messages were passed to them and they made their way to the station. By the time they got there it would be too late. He would have to pick up a crew as best he could on the way.

This he did. Fortunately his second coxswain had foreseen trouble in this weather and was already at the boathouse. Motor Mechanic Evan Owens was on the spot as usual. He lives in a house just at the back of the life-boat station where the footpath leads down to the boathouse. But these were only two members of his complete crew. Not nearly enough to launch the life-boat in the conditions.

Shore helpers had gathered at the boathouse—the men who work the winch engine and fold back the doors of the boathouse and who help to run the ropes to the life-boat when she is being rehoused. Coxswain Evans recruited two of these helpers who volunteered to go with him. One of them, Mr Hugh Jones, had never been out on service in a life-boat before.

At midday the life-boat, which the coxswain had never handled before and with little more than half her normal crew, plunged down the slipway into the raging water. And it was raging. Wind speeds of 104 miles an hour were recorded on Anglesey that day, and the waves were sometimes twenty-five feet between trough and crest.

The vessel they went to help was a 500-ton coaster called the *Hindlea*. She had come from Manchester and was bound for Newport in Monmouthshire in ballast with a crew of eight. When the life-boat found her she was riding to her starboard anchor, but this was not holding on the shingly bottom and the *Hindlea* was dragging towards the shore.

On the shore people had gathered to watch the rescue. Not

that they saw very much. The wind was screaming off the sea, the spray was like a curtain in front of them and they had to crouch behind a wall out of the wind's tearing hands. One man, a photographer, got to his feet to take a photograph of the doomed ship. He weighed about sixteen stone, yet the wind bowled him over and sent him spinning across a field, helpless. But he got his photograph. When it was developed the print showed a mass of spray through which the top of the *Hindlea*'s mast could just be seen.

In this howling madness the life-boat drew near the *Hindlea*. She was swinging ninety degrees from side to side, her engines racing, and the anchor cable was constantly being whipped out of the water as the vessel pitched, making a seaward approach dangerous. In fact the whole situation was dangerous in the extreme.

The life-boat stood by for nearly an hour and a half in wild seas. They could not take off the crew until the master gave the order to abandon ship, and masters of vessels are naturally loth to give such an order until there is no hope left. But this delay makes the act of rescue when it comes twice as difficult.

At last the master of the *Hindlea* gave up the unequal struggle and gave the order to abandon ship. By now she was only two hundred yards away from the rocks, inside the five fathom line. There was no hope for her now. Coxswain Evans described the water round her as 'a boiling mass of confusion', and when life-boat coxswains, who without exception have a gift for understatement, use phrases like that, the conditions must indeed have been appalling.

Coxswain Evans took the life-boat round the stern of the *Hindlea*, in great danger from the thrashing propeller which was now so high out of the water that it was churning above the heads of the life-boat crew, and as he brought her up on the port side the life-boat was hit by a tremendous sea which heeled her right over and put her mast under water. No boat, even a life-boat, could surely stand that treatment. For a moment she wallowed hesitantly and then came upright.

Another danger was growing. Further out to sea a tanker, *Essar I*, was also in difficulties, and unless the life-boat crew managed to get the crew of the *Hindlea* off in reasonably quick time there was a chance that this tanker, thousands of tons of helpless, perhaps inflammable material, might drift down on them before the gale.

Coxswain Evans approached the *Hindlea*. He wanted to have a trial run in alongside her before he gave the order to the *Hindlea*'s crew to jump. He drew in towards the port-quarter, and as he did so another enormous sea overtook the life-boat, lifted her up and very nearly landed her on the *Hindlea*'s deck which was more than ten feet above her waterline. As the sea withdrew again the life-boat dropped and struck the side of the *Hindlea* so hard that Coxswain Evans was sure she must be seriously damaged. But this did not prevent him from carrying on with his attempted rescue. For all he knew water might be pouring into her. Her fuel tanks might be ruptured. She might have burst so many of the air cases which kept her buoyant that she would sink in a very short time.

He went astern, clear of that dreadful heaving propeller, and ran in again. As he drew near the *Hindlea*'s side, calling orders to his motor mechanic and the second coxswain who was acting as assistant motor mechanic to manœuvre the engines to counteract the sea, one member of the crew jumped. Again Coxswain Evans went astern and ran in once more. Ten times in all he made that fearful run in with the pounding seas round the life-boat and the *Hindlea* drawing nearer and nearer the rocks on the shore. Each time he ran alongside another member of the crew jumped, until shortly after two o'clock all eight members had been taken off. In spite of the difficulties and dangers in the conditions, only one man was injured. He had broken his ankle.

The life-boat returned to Moelfre with the survivors, and the crew were prepared to eat their words about the life-boat they had been using. She may not have been beautiful to look at, but she had righted herself after dipping her mast in the water, she was still sailing well after that almighty jar she had taken against the *Hindlea*'s side, and she had handled better than the coxswain had ever hoped she would. In those conditions it was just as well. She had truly proved herself a life-boat.

Coxswain Evans was awarded the gold medal for this

rescue, the second such award since the end of the war. Motor Mechanic Evan Owens received the silver medal and the three other members of the life-boat's little crew were awarded bronze medals.

'So we brought them back,' said Coxswain Evans simply, as though they had been returning from a picnic. 'But that wasn't the end of it. I hardly had time to scrape the salt off my eyes before we were called out again.'

They went to the help of the tanker which had been in difficulties earlier. On her way to her the life-boat had to plough through the wreckage which was already spreading from the *Hindlea*. The Moelfre life-boat took turns with the Beaumaris life-boat in standing by the tanker for the following twenty-four hours, so the crew did not see the *Hindlea*'s end.

Watchers on the shore saw the *Hindlea* strike soon after the last man was taken off. They watched the enormous might of the sea lift off hatches and tanks and throw them into the air in ghastly fits of titanic madness. Steel plates were torn from her as though they had been matchwood, and some of them were found afterwards wrapped round rocks on the shore as though some clumsy giant has been trying to tie untidy paper parcels. It was facing seas of such fury that the Moelfre life-boat saved eight men from almost certain death.

CHAPTER SIXTEEN

Portrush—1960

In many life-boat stations it is possible to trace family connexions through several generations. It is not unusual to find whole families serving in the life-boat. Sometimes this situation has been brought about by the fact that in the old days the population at some life-boat stations was so small that almost every able-bodied man served the life-boat in one capacity or another. In the days of pulling and sailing life-boats crews were much bigger than they are now, and the consequent demand for members of the crew was greater. In many places the whole population, men, women and children of all ages, would turn out to help launch the life-boat. Manning the life-boat was often a family affair, as can be seen in the Ballycotton service to the Daunt Rock lightship where every member of the crew had the surname of Sliney or Walsh. Likewise at Cromer, during the *English Trader* rescue eight members of the crew of eleven had the surname Davies.

It seems in some places to be a tradition handed down from father to son to serve in the life-boat. This is not unnatural, especially in the small fishing villages where most people earn their living from the sea in any case and know its dangers.

A story which illustrates this family connexion happened at Caister in Norfolk.

A vessel had run aground on the Barber Sands on 13 November 1901, and in response to the distress flares she burnt, the life-boat had been launched in appalling conditions. The gale was blowing straight on to the beach, and most of the scores of people who had struggled to get the life-boat launched had gone home to change their soaked clothing, for many of them had been working up to their necks in the sea. But one man who waited on the shore for the return of the life-boat was James Haylett, a man of seventy-eight who had formerly been second

coxswain on the Caister life-boat. He stayed because on board
the life-boat were his two sons—one of them was the coxswain—
his son-in-law, and a grandson.

Standing there on the storm-swept beach old James Haylett
had refused many offers of shelter and warmth, and firmly
stayed where he was. For an hour he stood there in the freezing
cold, facing the fury of the gale, and then suddenly he saw the
life-boat loom out of the darkness near the shore.

At the same time as he saw the life-boat the men on the life-
boat saw the shore, and the coxswain desperately tried to turn
her away. But it was too late. The life-boat struck the sand with
such force that she capsized, pinning most of her crew underneath her. James Haylett called for help, and in spite of his
years he waded into the sea to lend what help he could. One of
his grandsons came to help him. Together they dragged one
man through the breakers on to the beach. It was James
Haylett's son-in-law. Then again they waded into the water and
returned with another man—his grandson. Yet again they
waded in and returned with a third man. James Haylett had
been almost swept out to sea by the strength of the waves and
drowned, and now he could do no more. The three men he and
his grandson had rescued were the only survivors of a crew of
twelve, and amongst those who died were James Haylett's two
sons.

There was an inquest and, trying to discover the reason for
the disaster, the coroner questioned James Haylett, suggesting
that perhaps the life-boat was returning, having failed in her
mission to reach the wreck. James Haylett said, 'No, sir. Caister
men never turn back.'

This phrase, so simply uttered by a man who had spent his
life with the life-boat and who had lost his two sons in the
disaster, was to become famous all over the world, and still
stands as an example of the spirit of the life-boat service.

But although members of the same family may serve in the
life-boat, the service is also manned by men who do not earn
their living from the sea. On the Isle of Wight the Brooke life-
boat had as coxswain a man who was a lawyer, soldier and
politician, and who became Secretary of State from 1912 to
1914. He was Major-General J. E. B. Seely, first Baron Mottis-

tone. When his other duties permitted he served with the life-boat for forty-two years, the last three of them as coxswain, until the station was closed in 1937.

Many others have served and continue to serve in the life-boats who earn their livings from other sources.

On Friday 21 October 1960 the Greek motor vessel *Argo Delos* left Glasgow for Cuba. She was in ballast and was to load sugar in Cuba after which she was bound for China.

The *Argo Delos* was a new ship. She had been built in Rotterdam eighteen months before, and her master, Captain Halamantis, had flown from Greece the previous week to take command of her. She was of 10,392 gross registered tonnage and was one of the finest vessels of the Greek Karas Line.

She had hardly started on her journey when disaster struck her. In bad weather and high seas she went aground on Torr Beg, a rocky islet about a mile north-west of Inishtrahull Island where the most northerly of the Irish lighthouses is situated.

Early on Saturday morning her distress signals were picked up by the Royal Navy frigate *Leopard* which was on exercise thirty miles off Islay in the Inner Hebrides. The *Leopard* immediately sailed to give what help she could.

The Malin Radio Station also picked up the *Argo Delos*'s distress call and passed it on to the coastguard at Portrush, which lies twenty-four miles away from Inishtrahull. The coastguard immediately told the honorary secretary of the Portrush life-boat station.

The maroons summoned the crew who gathered in the darkness at the life-boathouse. There was a strong breeze blowing from the south-east and the sea looked fairly rough. Furthermore, weather conditions were clearly getting worse and the forecast was not encouraging.

Mr Sam Cunningham is clerk to the Portrush District Council. His father held this same position for 46 years, and Mr Cunningham has a brother who is clerk to the Portstewart Council near by, so there is a family tradition here. But Mr Cunningham has another and very different job. He is coxswain of the Portrush life-boat.

The life-boat stood ready in the boathouse, its bows pointing towards the sea. The crew hurried into their boots and oilskins and at five minutes past three the life-boat ran down the slipway outside the boathouse, entered the water with a mountainous crash of foam, and Coxswain Cunningham steered her towards Inishtrahull.

The life-boat ran before the heavy seas as she made her way north-westwards, through the grey, wild October night, and two and a half hours after leaving her station she made contact with H.M.S. *Leopard*, which by then had reached the crippled ship and was standing by.

As dawn broke greyly over the angry sea the life-boat approached the *Argo Delos*, and the coxswain and the crew saw for the first time the situation she was in. She was grounded fore and aft, her bows on a rock and her stern on Torr Beg itself. The sea was crashing hungrily over her bows. It was a tricky situation.

Coxswain Cunningham took the life-boat to the lee side of the *Argo Delos*, but found that there was dangerously little clear water there, and the tide was swirling under the midships section of the vessel—which was not aground—at a rate of three knots. The approach would have to be made from the weather side—the starboard.

Coxswain Cunningham formed his plan, and over the radio-telephone informed the captain of the *Leopard* what he intended to do. On the loud hailer he tried to explain to the captain and crew of the *Argo Delos*, but no one on board seemed to speak or to understand English.

The captain of the *Leopard* agreed with the coxswain that in the conditions a rescue by life-boat was more likely to succeed than an attempt by a helicopter, but the *Argo Delos* was flooding internally and had no electric power, so communication with her was impossible. Therefore a naval party was landed on her deck with a portable radio-telephone, for it was important to have communication between the *Argo Delos* and the *Leopard*.

Before this, however, Coxswain Cunningham had managed to make the crew of the *Argo Delos* understand that they would have to rig a ladder at the after deck for the crew to climb down, and this was eventually done. He made three dummy runs to be sure in his own mind of the best way of taking off the crew, and at a quarter past eight he made his first real run in. This preparation was necessary, for the sea round the vessel was very confused and the life-boat was rising and falling fifteen feet at the *Argo Delos*'s side.

The crew passed down two boat ropes as the life-boat came alongside, one on each side of the ladder, and these were quickly attached to the life-boat, but before anyone could attempt to get off the vessel the ropes parted and the life-boat had to withdraw.

The crew of the *Argo Delos* rigged longer ropes and the life-boat ran alongside again. Four men came down the ladder and jumped for the life-boat. The second man mis-timed his jump and fell into the sea between the vessel and the life-boat, but he was quickly hauled aboard with nothing worse than an injured elbow.

While doing all this Coxswain Cunningham had to manœuvre the life-boat very carefully. There were rocks at the *Argo Delos*'s stern, so he could not slide in alongside. He had to approach the vessel head on and swing round hard to starboard when he was a few feet from the *Argo Delos*'s side. Then he had to manœuvre his port engine to keep the life-boat alongside and within jumping distance.

Each member of the crew came down the ladder one at a time, and when the coxswain shouted to him to do so he jumped backwards into the waiting arms of two of the life-boat's crew. The ropes parted again and again while this was being done, and three times Coxswain Cunningham had to move away from the *Argo Delos*'s side and come in again.

Fourteen men were taken off in an hour and three-quarters, and as time went by the operation became more and more difficult, for oil was leaking from the *Argo Delos*'s damaged hull, spraying over the life-boat and making the deck as slippery as a skating rink, and a skating rink which never stood still for a moment.

The only rope left now was a composite rope with a wire heart, and this was passed between the vessel and the life-boat. But as the life-boat dropped into the trough of the sea her weight pulled so hard on the rope that the bollard to which the rope was attached was jerked, some of the life-boat's planking was lifted and two of her deck beams were damaged. She had already suffered some other damage through being crashed against the *Argo Delos*.

After the fourteen men had been taken off a rope fouled the propeller and the port engine became useless. Coxswain Cunningham had needed both engines to get alongside the *Argo Delos*, and with only the starboard engine left active this was no longer possible, so he headed for the *Leopard* and transferred the rescued men to her.

Then he took the life-boat to the lee of a rock west of Inishtrahull, and in the calmer water there the engines could be stopped, the hatch lifted and the rope round the port propeller freed. The life-boat then stood by while a helicopter took off fifteen more members of the *Argo Delos*'s crew and transferred them to the *Leopard*. Each man was lifted from the deck of the crippled vessel and carried, still hanging in the harness below the helicopter, across the stormy water to the *Leopard* a mile away.

Then the life-boat left to return to her station. She had been on service for more than fourteen hours. Captain Halamantis and three other members of his crew were taken off during the next two days by helicopter, and soon afterwards the *Argo Delos* became a total wreck.

Coxswain Cunningham was awarded the silver medal for this service and Second Coxswain Robert MacMullan was awarded the bronze medal. He had stayed on duty on the slippery, oil-covered deck of the life-boat throughout the entire operation. And the captain, officers and ship's company of H.M.S. *Leopard* presented each member of the life-boat's crew with an engraved silver tankard in recognition of a feat of seamanship which deeply impressed the Royal Navy.

The Port St Mary life-boat stands by to take the keepers from the burning Chickens Rock lighthouse. See chapter XVII

Ham Voe, the only landing place on Foula, where the 52-foot life-boat had to lie during a gale. See chapter XVIII

The St Peter Port, Guernsey, life-boat lands a sick woman. A type of service described in chapter XVIII

CHAPTER SEVENTEEN

Port St Mary—1960

Although rescue from shipwreck forms the bulk of the life-boat service's work, there are other aspects of it which are not so common but which are just as important.

We have already seen something of the rescue by the Bally-cotton life-boat from the Daunt Rock lightship, but this really falls under the heading of rescue from shipwreck. Many of the lighthouses round our coast and all the lightships are cut off from direct land communication, and often emergencies arise which mean that the life-boats have to be launched. Besides the Daunt Rock lightship there was the more recent service to the North Carr lightship off Fife Ness by the Broughty Ferry life-boat which resulted in the loss of the life-boat and her entire crew. But sometimes it is not the lightship which requires attention. It is the men who man it. If a member of a lighthouse or lightship crew falls ill or is injured it is often the life-boat which is called either to take medical help out or to bring the sick or injured man back to the mainland.

Occasionally, however, it is both the men and the lighthouse which require help.

One of the outstanding examples of this type of service took place on the Isle of Man.

On either side of the neck of a peninsula at the south-west end of the Isle of Man stand two small villages. The westerly one is Port Erin and the easterly one is Port St Mary. Just off the tip of this peninsula lies a little island called the Calf of Man, and to the south-west of this island there is a reef of rocks on which stands the Chickens Rock lighthouse.

It is an odd name for a lighthouse, but it was so called by the old sailors who knew these seas well. On the rocks perch hundreds of storm petrels, the little ocean birds which rarely

come ashore except at nesting time. Storm petrels are sometimes known as Mother Carey's Chickens, and that is how the
lighthouse got its name when it was built nearly ninety years
ago.

The rocks over which the lighthouse stands sentinel are a
hazard to the busy shipping lanes round the south of the Isle of
Man. At low tide parts of the reef are uncovered, but for the
most part the rocks lie just below the surface waiting hungrily
for any unwary ship to pass over them. The sea is often angry
round the reef, churned into a boiling mass by the sharp, jagged
rocks. The tapering finger of the lighthouse is 143 feet high, a
slim, lonely tower in the midst of the sea. The lighthouse is
manned by a crew of three, and for eighty-five years the light
flashed its warning message into the darkness or the fog signal
echoed over the water when fog spread its silent hand over the
sea. Holidaymakers on the Isle of Man know the Chickens Rock
lighthouse well. From the shore it can be seen rising sheer from
the sea, and at night the rhythmic flash of its light every half
minute brings a sense of comfort and security even to those safe
ashore.

But on 23 December 1960 the Admiralty flashed a warning
to all shipping:

'The Chickens Rock Light has been extinguished and the fog
warning is not—repeat not—operating.'

A rare and unusual warning. It takes a real catastrophe for
the Admiralty to have to issue such a message. What had happened to make it necessary?

It was at half-past ten on that morning two days before
Christmas that disaster struck the Chickens Rock lighthouse.

Suddenly and without warning a violent explosion rocked
the lighthouse and within minutes the lantern house was ablaze.
The keepers were trapped. They were in one of the upper rooms
and the flames prevented them from getting downstairs to the
lower part of the lighthouse.

As the flames climbed slowly and hungrily towards them the
keepers rigged a rope from the upper balcony where they were
imprisoned, and one by one they slid down it, one hundred feet
to the base of the lighthouse. One of the men burnt his hands
badly as he slid down.

But this was only temporary safety. They had escaped the fire—now they were in danger from the sea. The tide was rising, and when it was full there would hardly be room for the three men to shelter. There was a strong wind blowing and the sea was very rough. As the tide rose the three men could be washed off the rock. The lighthouse was blazing steadily and inside were the fuel storage tanks which supplied the light, and if the fire reached these the whole building could go up in one blinding explosion. The keepers had been taken completely by surprise, and in the bitter cold and biting spray they were dressed only in shirts and trousers.

For them it was a desperate situation and the outlook was grim indeed.

And then through the mist and spray they caught sight of something which set their hearts leaping with hope. A small boat was tossing its way towards them, a boat painted in the familiar colours of red, blue and white, and on board they could see men dressed in the distinctive yellow oilskins and sou'westers of the Royal National Life-boat Institution.

The Port St Mary life-boat was coming to their aid.

The message had come to the honorary secretary from the coastguard at ten minutes past eleven. At that time it was not clear what the situation was at the lighthouse, but the crew assembled and the life-boat, which lies afloat, was prepared to leave. Shortly afterwards another message came to say that the keepers were in great danger. The life-boat *R. A. Colby Cubbin No. 2* slipped her moorings half an hour after the first message came through.

When the life-boat approached the lighthouse the keepers had retreated before the advancing tide to a small landing stage and the water was now swirling only a few feet below them.

The state of the sea and the hidden rocks round the base of the lighthouse made it impossible for the life-boat to approach nearer than a hundred yards. Coxswain Gawne decided to fire a line to the men, but this was difficult because there was nowhere the line could be fired to. In the heaving sea and with the strong wind it would be impossible to fire a line from the gun so that the keepers could catch it. But it had to be tried.

Over the loud-hailer the coxswain asked the keepers to stream a line attached to a board. This they did. They attached a piece of board to a length of line and threw the board into the sea. The movement of the tide carried the board away, streaming the line behind it while the keepers made their end of the line fast.

A line was fired from the life-boat. The crew watched it snaking out from its metal container, curving through the grey sky to splash into the sea over and beyond the line the keepers had streamed. The keepers hauled the line attached to the board in again, bringing the gun line in with it, and they were able to pick up the line from the life-boat.

The block was drawn over and the keepers made it fast to an iron ladder at the base of the lighthouse, and a breeches buoy was sent over from the life-boat.

The keeper who had burnt his hands was in the most need of attention, so the other two keepers strapped him into the breeches buoy and the life-boat crew began to haul him over the water towards the life-boat.

But when the man was half-way between the lighthouse and the life-boat a heavy sea capsized the breeches buoy and the man was flung into the water. The life-boat crew dragged him towards the life-boat and managed to pull him in. They wrapped him in a blanket and got him into shelter near the warmth of the life-boat's engines. He was now suffering badly from shock and exposure, and the coxswain decided it would not be possible to take off the other keepers this way. Wind, tide and the way the sea was running would endanger the lives of the two keepers waiting to be rescued if such an attempt were made.

A hasty radio message went out from the life-boat, requesting the nearby Port Erin life-boat to launch and come to stand by in case the two remaining keepers should urgently need help. The Port Erin life-boat *Matthew Simpson* was launched from her slipway immediately, and the Port St Mary life-boat made for Port Erin to land the injured keeper who clearly required medical attention.

An Air Force helicopter on Anglesey answered an urgent summons and flew to the Chickens Rock, but the pilot could see that it would be impossible for the keepers to climb through the flames and smoke to the upper balcony of the lighthouse again, and this was the only point from which a helicopter could lift them off. The only hope of saving the keepers lay with the life-boats . . .

From a hill on the Isle of Man a crowd of people gathered silently in twos and threes in the damp greyness of that day and stared out at the lighthouse which was a landmark they knew so well. They could see smoke billowing from the windows and they could see the white seas breaking round the base of the lighthouse. They were powerless to help, but the thoughts of every one of them were with the two stranded men and the two tiny boats which were trying to save them from the twin dangers of sea and fire.

Meanwhile the two keepers cowered on their scanty perch while the sea licked hungrily round their feet. The fire was still blazing in the lighthouse immediately above them, and no one knew whether it would reach the fuel tanks or not.

Shortly after three o'clock the Port St Mary life-boat returned to the Chickens Rock, and the two life-boats stayed tossing in the storm-swept water for over three hours before the weather moderated and the tide receded sufficiently to allow another attempt at rescue to be made.

While the Port Erin life-boat stood by, the Port St Mary life-boat edged cautiously through the broken water amongst the hidden rocks round the base of the lighthouse and came alongside. The two keepers were taken off. They had been exposed on the reef of rock for more than eight hours, half dressed, while the spray from the sea broke over them. Both men were in the last stages of exhaustion, badly burnt and suffering severely from shock and exposure. They were wrapped in blankets and put near the life-boat's engine for warmth, and then the two life-boats drew away from the still smoking stalk of the light-house and headed for home.

And that night the Chickens Rock lighthouse sent out no warning beam. Wisps of smoke still curled lazily from the soot-blackened windows and the empty shell stood stark and lonely on the reef which it had guarded for eighty-five years.

Two days later the Commissioners of Northern Lights' relief ship *Hesperus*, which had sailed from Oban, fixed a flashing beacon near the empty lighthouse as a temporary warning to shipping, for it would take some time to repair the lighthouse from which the three keepers had had such a hairsbreadth escape.

CHAPTER EIGHTEEN

Aith—1962

There are other calls made on the life-boat service which are not associated with saving life from the sea.

On many occasions ships put out emergency calls because a member of their crew has been taken ill and either needs to be taken to hospital or the services of a doctor. On these occasions the life-boat will take the patient ashore or land a doctor on board, for these calls often come when the ship is in such a position that it would take too long to reach a port.

One of the most unusual services performed by a life-boat took place on 9 October 1959. There had just been a General Election, and all over the country the ballot boxes had to be collected. Round the western isles of Scotland, however, the weather was very bad, and somehow the ballot boxes on the little island of Colonsay had to be brought to the mainland to be counted. There was no vessel available for this purpose and the Islay life-boat was asked to help. The *Charlotte Elizabeth* left her moorings at Port Askaig in the Sound of Islay and headed northwards to Colonsay. The ballot boxes were duly collected and the life-boat returned to her station, having been at sea for over seven hours.

The life-boats round the west coast of Scotland and in the Orkney and Shetland Islands perform a type of service not normally performed by life-boats. The stations at Barra Island, Islay, Stornoway; Longhope, Stromness and Stronsay on Orkney and at Aith and Lerwick on Shetland between them cover the range of islands ringing the coast at this point. Mallaig and Thurso, the only stations on the mainland, also cover these islands.

Thick fog shrouded the Inner Hebridean islands of Islay, Jura and Colonsay on 24 June 1960, and it was at this time that a woman fell ill on Islay and urgently needed hospital attention. The Air Ambulance service which operates to all these islands from Renfrew Airport near Glasgow was unable to get through owing to the bad visibility, and the local medical officer asked for the service of the life-boat. The life-boat was prepared immediately, the patient and doctor taken aboard at Port Askaig, and the life-boat sailed for Oban on the mainland, a distance of about fifty miles, through thick fog between a chain of islets and rocks, and landed the patient safely.

A similar service was performed further north eighteen months later, but this time the weather conditions were different.

Some twenty miles to the west of the mainland of Shetland lies the island of Foula, perhaps the loneliest inhabited island round the coast of Britain. It is a grim, inhospitable, rocky island, little more than two miles across at any point, and on many occasions during the long, dark northern winter the island is cut off from the mainland by storm and wind. Sometimes the inhabitants never see anyone from the outside world for weeks at a time. Food and paraffin run short, and the island is swept by the enormous Atlantic waves and the wind tears across Foula with fantastic force. The island life is hard and not to be undertaken by the physically weak. Yet, in the nature of things, people do fall ill.

The nearest life-boat station to Foula is at Aith on the Shetland mainland. The most northerly of Britain's life-boat stations, Aith is a tiny village situated at the southern end of Aith Voe, a sheltered arm of the sea. Here the 52-foot Barnett-type life-boat *John and Frances Macfarlane* lies at her moorings, a new boat, and one of the biggest of the life-boat fleet, for, like Lerwick on the opposite side of the mainland, she may have vast distances to cover along that lonely, dangerous coastline.

Much of the Aith life-boat's work is concerned with Papa Stour—a small island just off the mainland—and with Foula. Frequently emergencies arise on one or other of these islands and only the life-boat is capable of getting through.

There is no doctor on either Papa Stour or Foula. The nearest doctor lives at Walls which is about an hour's car journey away from Aith.

This story is typical of the work done by the Aith life-boat station, which must be one of the loneliest in Britain.

It was at ten minutes to seven on the evening of 8 February 1962 that the doctor at Walls received a telephone call from the nurse on Foula saying that a woman on the island had been taken seriously ill, urgently needed medical attention and should be taken to hospital as soon as possible.

The doctor promised to do what he could, and as he replaced the telephone receiver he glanced out of his window. Frequent furious squalls of snow and sleet battered at the window and the wind was blowing hard from the west-south-west—almost directly from Foula, and any vessel attempting to make the passage would be sailing directly into the teeth of the gale.

The doctor rang the honorary secretary of the Aith life-boat station. In view of the weather and the seriousness of the patient's condition, the life-boat was placed at his disposal. The doctor immediately got into his car and began the journey to Aith across the windswept, desolate moorland.

That distant voice on the telephone from Foula was having its effect. Already over the dark, stormswept mainland people were stirring in answer to the call for help. The hospital in Lerwick was alerted. An ambulance set out for Aith to collect the sick woman, and Coxswain Robert Anderson, who was awarded the Distinguished Service Medal during the war for his work on minesweepers, summoned the crew of the life-boat by maroons. When the doctor arrived at Aith at eight o'clock he was taken out to the life-boat immediately in the boarding boat.

At ten minutes past eight the life-boat left her moorings.

The weather was getting worse and the life-boat faced a long and gruelling passage. It was twenty-seven miles from Aith to Foula, and in normal conditions the life-boat could cover the distance in something over three hours, but her passage took her through the narrow Sound of Papa, between the mainland and Papa Stour. This was a dangerous journey at the best of times, for there were no lights on Papa Stour to guide the boat. A radio-telephone message from the coastguard confirmed that the weather was getting worse. Coxswain Anderson posted men as look-outs and reduced speed as he passed through the Sound of Papa. Visibility was so bad that despite the urgency of the call he dared not go any faster.

The life-boat came through the Sound safely and met the full force of the wind and sea as she cleared the mainland.

Meanwhile the honorary secretary rang through to Foula and asked for a lamp to be placed on the pier to assist the life-boat to make her landfall. This was promised.

There is only one landing place on Foula—Ham Voe on the east side of the island. It is a small inlet with very little depth of water and a reef of rock lying opposite the tiny pier, which makes manœuvring a 52-foot life-boat a difficult operation even under normal conditions, and the water is so shallow at the inner end of the pier that the life-boat cannot lie full length at it.

At about one o'clock in the morning, through the solid wall of darkness ahead, the look-outs on the life-boat picked up the tiny flicker of light on the pier. The journey had so far taken nearly five hours instead of the normal three, and the most difficult part still lay ahead—guiding the life-boat into the tiny inlet through the heavy seas, with nothing to steer by except that one point of light. The coxswain began to steer towards it, but even as he did so the light suddenly went out. The only guide in to Ham Voe had disappeared.

Foula had been cut off for so long that stocks of paraffin had almost entirely gone, and the lamp on the pier had failed for lack of fuel. However, the landing had to be made, and sailing almost blind the coxswain took the life-boat in towards the inlet. As he did so tiny flickering lights appeared again to guide him in. They came from hand torches, and the pinpricks which they made in the darkness enabled the coxswain to guide the life-boat in to Ham Voe. The life-boat was at last made fast at the pier at a quarter past two in the morning after six hours of buffeting through appalling conditions. The doctor was put ashore and taken to the patient.

He had to spend some time on the island, treating her and preparing her for the journey which in those conditions would be a taxing one for a sick woman. While they waited there was no rest for the crew of the life-boat. There is little shelter in Ham Voe and the constant surge of the angry sea and the pull of the tide kept the crew busy protecting their boat from being battered against the pier. At last the doctor reappeared with a stretcher party. The sick woman was strapped to the stretcher and she and the doctor were taken aboard the life-boat at six o'clock in the morning. A quarter of an hour later the life-boat sailed for home. The seas were still very heavy, but daylight was approaching and visibility began to improve, and with the wind behind her the life-boat made good progress. She arrived back at Aith at half-past nine. An ambulance was waiting and the patient was transferred to it and taken to hospital at Lerwick twenty miles away across the mainland.

Despite the buffeting the life-boat had received on her passage and during the four hours she had been lying at the pier at Ham Voe, she had suffered practically no damage, which reflects not only great credit on the builders of the boat but also on the superb seamanship of the coxswain and the crew who had sailed through those terrible northern seas for nine hours to save the life of a sick woman on Foula.

CHAPTER NINETEEN

Postscript

The stories which have made up this book are mostly spectacular ones and may serve to show the conditions and dangers which the life-boatmen are called upon to face. But not all their work is so dramatic although it is almost always as arduous. Much of the life-boats' time is taken up with fruitless searches, the result of strange lights seen at sea by the coastguards, or by messages which may later prove incorrect or even false, but these signs can never be ignored. If there is the remotest chance of anyone requiring assistance the life-boat is there to help, and if on many occasions the life-boat returns empty-handed this is all part of the service of watching over the safety of those who go to sea.

Sometimes the work is purely routine: fishing boats in trouble in sudden weather changes, and the life-boat has to stand by them until they safely regain the shelter of harbour; standing by a vessel which is in some temporary danger from the wind, weather, current or tide, but which later manages to withdraw from that danger.

A rather comical example of this was the case of a yacht in St Ives Bay. The people on board lit the Primus stove for a cup of tea. The Primus was turned up too high and there was a minor explosion. Scared of fire, the people on the yacht radioed urgently for help. The St Ives life-boat was launched and made for the yacht. When they reached her the Primus was working perfectly, there was no danger, and those on the yacht offered the life-boatmen a cup of tea. What the life-boatmen said is not on record.

But no life-boatman knows exactly what he is going to have to face when the call comes to launch. He may spend hours quartering an empty sea in the hope of finding a survivor from a crashed aircraft, or he may find himself involved in an epic struggle which will in the future colour the already colourful pages of the Institution's history. There is never any certainty about what he will face, except the fact that it will always be unpleasant and often dangerous, and that he will return home, sometimes after many hours, cold, wet, hungry and tired.

Nor does he know when the call will come. It may be during the day when he is at work or during the night when he is asleep, and a life-boatman usually sleeps with his boots at the foot of his bed if the weather is bad. It may come when he is in church and he will leave in the middle of the service, or it may come when he is sitting down to his Christmas dinner with his wife and children round him. The call may come at any time, and whenever it comes the life-boatman leaves whatever he is doing and makes for the boathouse.

And there are those who are left behind: the wives and mothers and sisters and children, who can only wait and listen to the wind and rain beating on the window panes, or who stand on the shore or the cliff top waiting for the approaching lights which will show that the life-boat is returning. Perhaps their ordeal is the worst of all, for they have nothing to occupy their hands and minds while the menfolk are away.

Yet the work goes on ceaselessly, day and night, year in, year out, and the record of lives saved mounts steadily. At almost all times somewhere round our coast a life-boat is at sea.

The cost of running such an organization is enormous and is increasing year by year. The first life-boat, Greathead's *Original*, cost £76 to build. The first pulling and sailing life-boat built by White's of Cowes cost £116. Today the cheapest life-boat costs £33,000, and the biggest Barnett life-boat costs nearly £50,000. A launching tractor costs £8,500. Life-boat repairs, maintenance of stations and equipment, awards to crews on service, all add up to the colossal cost of over a million pounds a year. And this money comes from the people. It comes from legacies of thousands and from the pennies put into collecting boxes on Flag Days. There is a vast team of voluntary labour all over the country which organizes the collection of this money, and through this money, freely given, the Institution is enabled to manage its own affairs without interference, quietly, calmly, efficiently and, above all, quickly. It is an organization which has been built up for nearly a hundred and fifty years, growing steadily in stature and strength, and with a reputation second to none throughout the world.

There is little room in such an organization for someone simply 'doing a job'. The inspiration of the Royal National Life-boat Institution is that it is run entirely by people whose sole aim, in whatever field of the Institution's work they find themselves, is the need to provide help and rescue for those in peril on the sea.

Bibliography

In writing this book I have been greatly helped by much local information provided by coxswains and honorary secretaries from all over England, Scotland, Wales, Northern Ireland, the Isle of Man and the Channel Islands, and information from the Institution's headquarters in London. Other papers and books which have been of great assistance are:

The Life-boat, the journal of the Royal National Life-boat Institution, published quarterly, 1915–1962.
The Life-boat and its Story. Noel T. Methley. Sidgwick & Jackson. 1913.
Launch! Major-General J. E. B. Seely. Hodder & Stoughton. 1932.
Modern Life-boats. J. R. Barnett. Blackie. 1933.
Storm on the Water. Charles Vince. Hodder & Stoughton. 1946.
The Life-boat Story. Patrick Howarth. Routledge & Kegan Paul. 1957.
Henry Blogg of Cromer. Cyril Jolly. Harrap. 1958.

Index

Index

Index